MW01714101

POETRY RIVALS 2011

FROZEN IN TIME

Edited by Jenni Bannister

First published in Great Britain in 2011 by:
Forward Poetry
Remus House
Coltsfoot Drive
Peterborough
PE2 9BF
Telephone: 01733 890099
Website: www.forwardpoetry.co.uk

All Rights Reserved
Book Design by Spencer Hart & Tim Christian
© Copyright Contributors 2011
SB ISBN 978-1-84418-582-5

FOREWORD

In 2009, Poetry Rivals was launched. It was one of the biggest and most prestigious competitions ever held by Forward Poetry. Due to the popularity and success of this talent contest like no other, we have taken Poetry Rivals into 2011, where it has proven to be even bigger and better than last year.

Poets of all ages and from all corners of the globe were invited to write a poem that showed true creative talent - a poem that would stand out from the rest.

We are proud to present the resulting anthology, an inspiring collection of verse carefully selected by our team of editors. Reflecting the vibrancy of the modern poetic world, it is brimming with imagination and diversity.

As well as encouraging creative expression, Poetry Rivals has also given writers a vital opportunity to showcase their work to the public, thus providing it with the wider audience it so richly deserves.

CONTENTS

THE POEMS

I LOVE SCHOOL

School is my favourite place to go,
I love to see my friends and say hello.
I like to write and learn new things,
Some people just moan and whinge,
As the end of the day draws near
All the children laugh and cheer,
But for me I can't wait
As tomorrow at school will be just as great.

Chloe Day (9)

BECAUSE I LOVE

Because I love,
Flowers will bloom and grow around me.
Because I love,
Others will love me too.

Because I love,
Everyone will be safe.
Because I love,
People will achieve their goals.

Because I love,
Dreams of innocent children will come true.
Because I love,
People that live on the streets nationwide will have a warm loving home.

Because I love,
All people will be clothed.
Because I love,
There will be a working cure to fight cancer and other serious medical conditions.

Because I love,
Everyone will have enough food.
Because I love,
Everyone will have enough clean water.

Because we love,
The world will live in union and peace.

Beth Eadon (11)

LITTLE THINGS

Monday is
Late alarms,
Wet hair,
Fresh clothes,
Burnt toast,
Waiting for the bus,
Exchanging weekend tales,
Missing assemblies,
Annie's ambushes,
James in French,
Elora at break,
Little things.
Tuesday is
Waking early,
Finishing homework,
Forgetting keys,
Wondering, 'Where on earth is the bus?'
Louis' humour,
Rushing to maths,
Telling Alex to stop poking us,
Not going to break,
Sitting at the stairs, reading, of course,
Laughter in history,
Little things.
Wednesday is
Pressing the 'snooze' button,
Running out of breakfast again,
Dog hair on my blouse,
Grabbing the keys on the way out,
Running for the bus today,
The Minta's (far too loud),
Sleeping in assembly,
Bored in English,
Skipping lunch,
Hazelgrove's hugs in games,
Little things.
Thursday is
Yawning awake,
Missing breakfast,
Shouting greetings,
Late buses,
Josh and Vee, arguing again,
Absent eavesdropping,

Remembering choir,
Losing keys,
Tripping on the stairs,
Frowning endlessly,
Little things.
Friday is
Holed tights,
Crumpled clothes,
Over-loaded with school things,
Bus is late again,
Tired smiles,
Josh and Vee, still arguing,
Curling up in the library,
Listening to music,
Aching headaches,
Watching the clock,
Little things.
Saturday is
Lie-ins, past breakfast,
Early lunch,
Walking the dog,
Jake, Georgia, Carlton Park,
Wandering home,
Blistered feet,
Worn pages,
Hot radiators,
Watching the stars,
Late to bed,
Little things.
Sunday is
Falling out of bed,
Feeding the dog,
Feeding the cat,
Broken shoes,
Going shopping,
Hanging out in happiness,
Running home in the rain,
Listening to thunder,
Counting 'elephants',
Falling asleep, smiling,
Little things.

The ones that make the world go round.

Gabriella King (12)

LOST GRANDFATHER

You were the best, the kindest, the smartest,
You were like a second father to me,
Every time I saw you my heart came to peace,
I was little so my memory of you isn't the best,
Seeing the photos makes me tremble in pain,
People told me I was your favourite,
You got me everything, my nappies, clothes, trainers, food, footballs,
But most importantly you gave me love,
Every time flicking through old albums my hand shakes,
I inhale oxygen, I get conscious of my breathing,
Frightened that I too will die,
I can't bear the fact of turning a page,
My heart will always have a place for you,
Your aroma still drifts in my brain,
Every night I get flashbacks of your face,
I don't know how you are but I wish I could,
Everything I do I look up the sky
As if you are gazing down at me watching my every move,
You have been with me through thick and thin,
Through my tough times, my great time,
I love you Grandfather no matter where you are,
You will always be my angel, my guardian,
Even when I take my last gasp of air I will still be with you.

Lindor Mehmetaj (14)

BUSY BEE

The bee is as stripy as a tiger,
As busy as an ant,
Busy bee collecting honey from the flowers,
Busy flying around the world collecting juicy amounts of honey from each delicious flower.
I love you busy bees collecting the honey.

Ellen Wolstenholme (6)

ODE TO THE WAR

Silent screams come with the hour
That you approach the field of the blood-red flower
The death cries of one thousand men,
Six decades on and yet your heart bleeds for them

Wounded and dying, lying in the mud,
The discharge of a gun, then the muffled thud,
Of bullet through flesh, the outcome of war,
Soldiers dying for us, so the future may soar

And as we remember the pain and the hell,
The blood and the tears, the lives they did sell
For our freedom and our families; those they would not know
We know why we're here, for it is the poppy seed we sow.

Izaak James Bailey (16)

MY HEAVEN

Is this my land?
A place that I can call my own?
The sun etching over my entire loved ones
Keeping us safe and sound.
They will always be with me and always around me here,
Never forgotten in my place where I will some time be.

A man watching over and smiling at me
He sees that I have done right and has shown me my path through life.
Helping when I have needed Him
And forgiving me when I have done wrong.

The perfect place,
Surrounded with the things and people I love,
The friendly warmth that shudders through my whole body
Knowing that this place is here,
A wondrous place that will carry me through my life,
Helping me to make the right decisions.

My Heaven will always be here!
My place, my land, my choices.

Naomi Claire Willmott (14)

ALONE

The night is loud,
Loud with the crowd,
Loud with people,
Who make me so feeble.
Helpless I am,
A poor little lamb,
Lost in the overwhelming cram.

I'm lost I admit,
From my family I have split.
How I got here I don't know,
But like everyone says, go with the flow.

No one at all seems to care,
No longer can I bear
The thought of being alone,
Alone, on my own.

I feel so tired,
Like my brain has been unwired.
Dizzy I feel,
Like a wheel.
Spinning round and round,
I'm lost but will I be found?

Ella Deighton (11)

BROTHER AND SISTER

My little brother likes to play,
and loves to kill people and be a pirate all day.
I like to dance and love to run,
I'll do it all day, it will bring me fun.
My brother likes to play games on the laptop;
the problem is when I need it he won't stop.
I like films and hate books,
I find it cool watching cooks.
But I will always be here for him and he will be here for me,
even if we're older we still won't flee.

Megan Reynolds (12)

BURNING CANDLE

Love is like a burning candle
Hey love burning through the night
Shining bright for all to see.
Like a sword it can hurt you, double lash,
Force of a knight shining bright for all to see,

Paint me a picture of love,
I will run this race, I will pay the price,
I will do all, paint me a picture of love
Because I can see this life is breaking us apart
But I still love you all the same.

I'm like a sad singer with no song,
I'm as happy as a butterfly that's unfurling its new wing,
I am as lonely as a beach in the depths of the winter,

But your character is like a candle
You try to cover but the smoke leaks out
And I see who you are
But I always know that there is light at the end of the tunnel,

Paint me a picture of love,
I will run the race, I will pay the price
And I still love you all the same.

Gift Ajimokun (12)

FUTURE

Who knows what the future holds
To be a pop star
To be a millionaire
Future is a mystic thing
To be a famous book writer
To be a master chef
Future is worth waiting for
To be a hairdresser
To be an actor
Your future will come true.

Abigail Dilley (9)

BROKEN HEART

We were just pretending,
Never really knowing
What was reality
And what was fantasy.

Now you're gone
And I'm alone
Wondering why,
We had to say goodbye.

You've no idea how much pain you've caused
Deep down my heart,
You don't care that I'm suffering
As you're the one that tore us apart.

If only you hadn't said goodbye,
I wouldn't be like this,
If you'd stayed by my side,
We would've had our first kiss.

Your reason to leave wasn't good enough,
Although I always knew,
That you didn't love me
As much as I loved you.

Levana Louise Hall (13)

GRANDPA (THE LAST BREATH)

So pale, so fragile,
Strained rising of his chest.
He used to be so agile,
Now he's falling into rest.

A cough, a splutter,
The anguish in those eyes.
Quietly spoken mutters,
A loved one's desperate cries.

The constant beep is silenced,
A chill takes over all.
With other worldly guidance,
They lift him from his fall.

Lydia Cullen (13)

A TROUBLED MIND

It's difficult to sleep on a troubled mind,
on a pained heart with its strings confined.
We toss and we turn and we yearn in our sleep,
but we lay, until day, finding nothing, we weep.

We cry on our pillows that always seem wet,
and mind always muddled, a constant mess where we fret.
The ceiling is daunting as it stares us down,
while we're simply wishing for that solace to be found.

The sun streams through poorly concealed blinds,
uncovering all and showing the world all its finds.
We hide under the duvet and pray in the dark,
the stains on our pillows our worldly mark.

There's a chatter outside in the street today,
where moms and dads walk and many a children play.
But I'm watching the clock, hearing the hands as they move,
heart beating fast, its soundtrack, the blues.

Frigid temperature, the scorching sun soon settles,
along with the fading of light and the pulling of petals.
And now is the time, where I am to sleep again,
but I'll lay awake, weep on my pillow, and wish I was in a world of pretend.

Chloe Sarie Kane (16)

DREAMS

I lay in bed dreaming,
Of princesses, magic and diamond rings gleaming.
Of far away lands where dragons roam
And a talking and walking real-life gnome!

I am lost in my fairy-tale fantasy,
My world of absolute simplicity.
With happy endings where good beats bad,
It's a place where no one's ever sad.

I'm distracted from the lurking danger,
Of evil witches, monsters and strangers.
This is where you should be aware,
Just in case you find a nightmare!

Katie Wright (13)

HURTING

My eyes are hurting
My legs are hurting
My hands are hurting
My arms are hurting me
My body is shaking
My head is aching
I am feeling killer pain causing me
I cannot move
My body is stuck
You said you didn't care about me
That is why I am so shocked
Why must you lie to me
And tell me you care?
When actually this is all just a dumb little game
Shivering in the cold
In a little corner
All dark with no light
All alone when nobody home
I want to cry . . . but I am emotionless
My eyes are hurting
My legs are crumbling
I cannot feel any pain
I cannot scream
Instead red teardrops I cry
He's taken it to the extreme.

Jana Hrubisova (14)

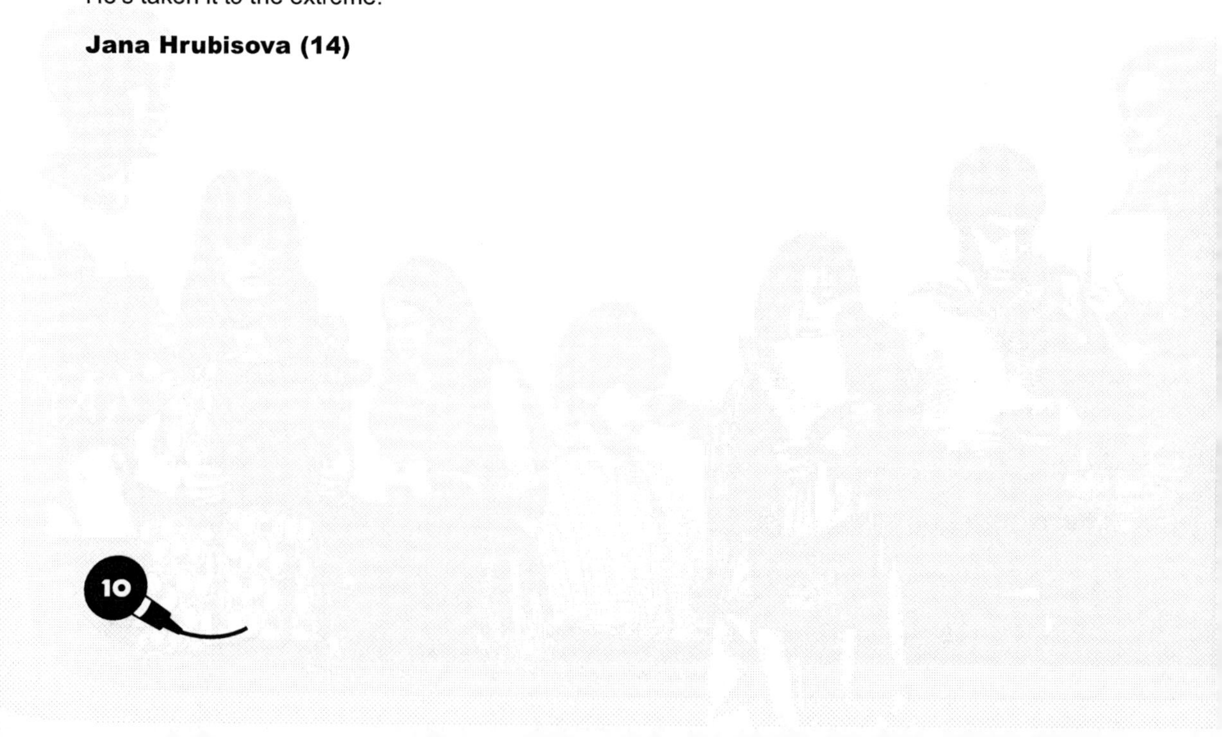

WHY DID YOU LEAVE ME?

Why did you leave me? You were once my friend,
Oh, why did you leave me?
Our friendship may end.

Oh, all the fun together will now be lost,
We didn't care about the weather,
Each other mattered the most.

As our friendship sign has made a depart,
It has broken my heart.

Why did you leave me? You were once my friend,
Oh, why did you leave me?
Our friendship may end.

I really don't know how I can take it,
Even if I had all the time,
I really don't know how I can make it,
Even if I tried to make our bond shine.

I've got to try and manage without you,
Make happiness come to life,
That's what I'll do.

I'll make it through,
Somehow.

The joy's been sucked out of me,
Got to try and stop myself from being unhappy.

Try to, try to, try to . . .
Look on the bright side,
Be ready to fight,
Make smiles appear on both of our faces,
Friendship and affection,
With the best of graces,
Someday, I'll find a way . . .

Rengoni Bhuyan (9)

MY HEART

My heart is like the halcyon sea,
moving calmly, slowly and free.

My heart is like the flying birds,
flying so quickly that they are not heard.

My heart is like a shining star,
you and me will never be apart.

My heart truly belongs to you,
our friendship really is true,
you're my best friend,
right till the end,
I hope you feel the same way too,
because I really do love you.

Grace Easlea (11)

INNOCENT

One man rips open the carriage door,
the innocent mother is called a whore.
Who these men are, she is unaware,
their arms reach and their eyes flare.
Fingers make an army of clenched fists,
a baby's cry is drowned within the midst.
Wrists are invaded, screams strain,
they all want empty bodies to remain.
From her car, the woman is extracted,
one more life will be subtracted.
Her headscarf is ripped by their hurricane,
for this reckless hatred, mothers are slain.
Her face is spat upon and her body battered,
blood oozes and the baby's future is shattered.

Roshni Deo (16)

OUR EARTH

For every little baby
That is born on our Earth
Another person dies
For every flower that blooms
And every bird that flies
There'll always be a couple more
That get shot up in their flight

For every drop of rain
That falls onto our Earth
A couple more will follow
To make a pattering sound
And more and more will keep on falling
As our Earth spins round and round

Every storm that brews
Might turn into a dreadful flood
For every gun that shoots
Will be followed by a gush of blood
Our Earth that we walk on every day
Is simply just a pile of mud

So for every step you take
On our Earth
And every wheel that turns
Try to be, a bit more cautious
Because you never know, what can lead to a crash and burn
But for every burn, a flame will always flicker
No matter big, or small

There are those who really care
About our Earth
And there are those, who sit alone in despair
But are they really alone?
Not to me, or anyone really
Because everyone will soon enough learn
That our Earth is not as happy
As we make it out to be.

Zara Rahman (13)

UNANSWERED QUESTIONS

Alcohol is the second biggest killer:
Why is life just not fair?
30,000 bulls are killed through bullfighting each year:
Why listen to things we cannot bear?
Kayapo people live in the Amazon Rainforest:
There are others out there but where?

Coal is non-renewable:
Why do we need to know?
The light from the sun is 8 minutes in the past:
Is there nowhere else for it to go?
Thou shall not kill
Then why do people sink so low?
Boycotting is a form of direct action:
Should we be made to sit in a row?

It is only male humpback whales that sing:
When is it our turn?
There are 120 frozen bodies on Mount Everest:
Why do these things make our stomachs churn?
Family is the main agent of socialisation:
Why should we have to learn?
King Edward I persecuted the Jews:
From that - what did he earn?

Chanice Rose Taylor (14)

SPRING

Spring has sprung,
The sun is up,
Just a little bump,
In the mornings birds are singing,
With the lovely breeze.

The sky is blue,
The clouds are white,
The trees are green,
The sky is bright.

Alice Burns (12)

THE MAGIC BOX

(Based on 'Magic Box' by Kit Wright)

I will put in my box . . .
The sweetest skies from Scandinavia
And a beautiful breeze brushing my face,
The sour sensation of sucking a lemon.

I will put in my box . . .
A book telling me his life story,
The wind of the north blowing the trees,
The wonderful wind whistling my ways.

I will put in my box . . .
Four happy children playing tennis together,
The last cough of a dying one
And a happy childhood ahead of me.

I will put in my box . . .
The 22nd century,
The soup in the chamber pot
And the pee in the pan.

My box is made from . . .
The water of life,
The yappiness of a puppy
And the smile of a newborn baby.

I will wish for no other toy,
Whilst I can play with this
And dream no other dream,
For my box is the centre of me.

Eleanor Kerr (9)

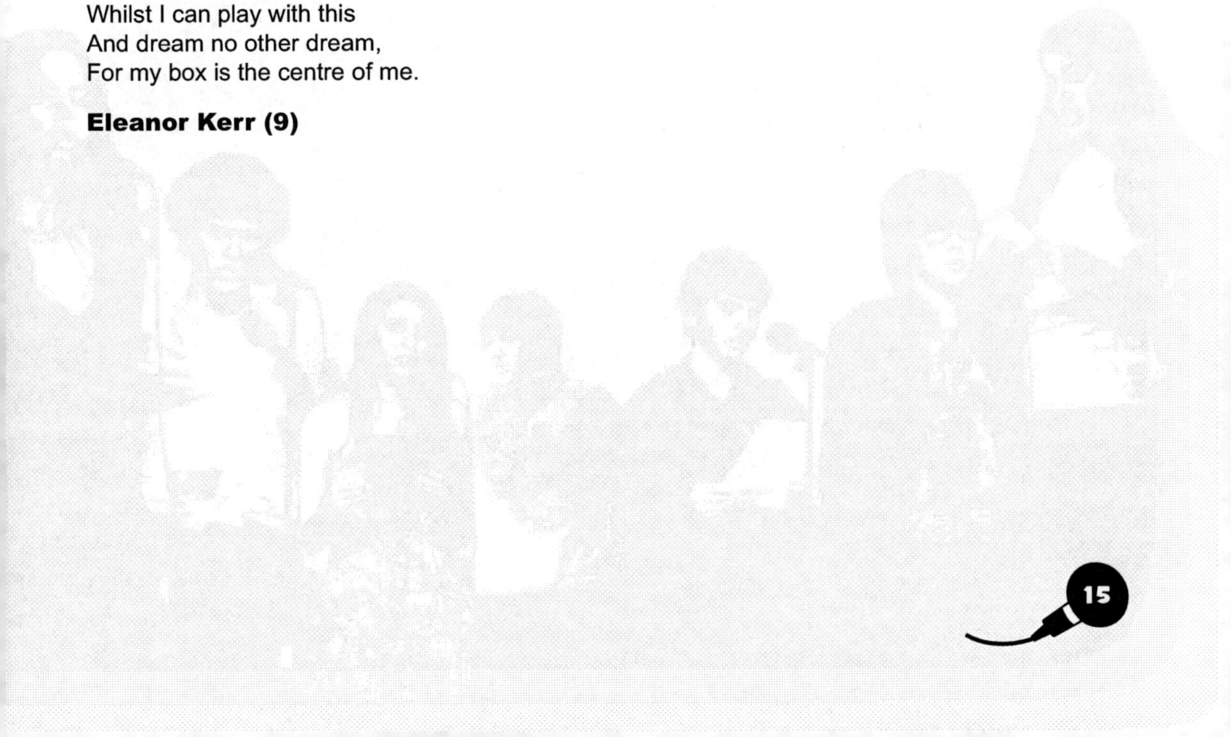

INFINITUS PHYSIKOS

Here, we are strange superfluities
Alive, able-bodied, but still no idea
Of an entire rationale of existence.

Here, we can qualm our reality
Assist when somebody has a fear
But still no idea, of the incessant caverns of the unknown.

There, naive innocents plummet into the preying snare
Of the hooded moths scrambling and screaming
Injecting their arbitrary units of conned phenomena.

From that impudent call of conflict
Came the waiting separation of fuming
Civilisations skirmishing with diverse fraudulent ideas of humanity.

Countless epiphanies anon . . .

Now, the perimeter breached and the truth is scared
A phenomenon with a scientia that's structuring,
Structuring an entire new understanding of the universal black.

Shadows afraid, light is coming,
A fresh nebula is on the verge of forming a star
No burning remnant though, a spark of genius
A patient discovery in the inter-dimensional heavens.

We're not leading a recline of false reality,
We are walking on the roof of a revolution
And the door is just waiting, waiting for the decent Einstein
To tremble on all quantum secrets that secrete in that breathing paradox
And connect with the unconnectable . . .

. . . before long, the impossible will be the probable.

Marcus Trinder (15)

THE COUNTRY I LOVE: MOROCCO

Morocco is a country of fun and delight,
The mosques, the shows; what a beautiful sight,
Advertisements are asking people to come
And I have got no shame in saying, 'That is where I am from!'

Fez is a city with vital history,
The oldest and first ever university,
The town which accommodates up to 45 degrees,
Due to the location of no surrounding seas.

Casablanca: well-known for its foreign movie,
This does not portray full amiability and beauty,
The mosque built for the former king's birthday,
This is known as mosque Hassan 2 today.

The food is unbeatable,
From couscous to tagines the residents say, 'Kol,'
This word means 'eat' in the Moroccan language,
At least you won't have to munch on a plain old sandwich!

So be grateful for the unique culture,
This may not be your everyday nature,
Homeless people still enjoying their lives,
A money donation is what keeps them alive
And you might see a homeless person,
But you might ignore them and merely bypass them.

Morocco is not a country where people go to die,
It's merely a peaceful country with death sublimed,
The residents there just work and relax,
No big deal about paying tax!

This should be the way in every country,
But the UN would never agree,
Just being greedy and wanting wealth,
Not caring but about themselves!

Farid El-Aouadi (12)

FOREVER ALONE

I don't know what to do
I've been here before
But only with you
Now that you are gone
I am singing this song
Forever alone

You made me happy
You made me sad
You made me feel like I was loved
Now I feel like a rock
Unloved and hard in the heart
Forever alone

Never knew what hate was
Until this very moment
When you blocked the path
To hope, to comfort, to love
Forever alone.

Rhiannon Grey (13)

FEARS

In the staunch darkness I wait
For my zealous feet to hit the ground,
Feeling time rush by in hate
I linger, caught on the edge of sound
While my fuelled fears ring untrue.

With the wind howling in my ears
The youthful cries sweep like tears down my face.
A stirring in my darkest fears
And my desperate hopes quicken pace,
My ravaged world pertaining to chaos.

It is true that I once felt,
Felt hope and love and happiness within,
But now for pain my heart does melt,
A withered organ fed by a twisted grin -
Am I too far gone to ask, 'What have I done?'

Caitlin Evans (16)

THE MASQUERADE BALL

Oh, she looks so pretty in that emerald gown
And the sapphire blue mask to hide the frown
That I couldn't see, oh silly me.

Take a dance through the exotic air of the night
It's raining outside but we don't fight
The weather, come stand under my umbrella.

The fireworks start and we glance up to the sky
Hold my hand and I swear we'll fly
Up into the stars, we'll never be apart.

Then a chill haunts the air and look to your eyes
What lies there comes as a huge surprise
But what kills me the most is the breach of my trust
A shining gold ring that crumbles to dust.

It falls to the ground, consumed by the dark
As we part with a final bitter embrace
I'm left with memories of your tearless face.

I watch as the tiger takes her hand
A whirlwind romance; a one night stand
That'll leave her with no one, get out, go, run.

I fall to the floor but I'm caught in their arms
Whispers that leave her with no second chance
But I'm a masochist - and she's my antagonist.

I feel their love and my eyes fly open
My tiger and maiden make me feel frozen
My own mask falls, I've lost it all

'Cause she looked so pretty in that torn raven gown
And without her mask I now see the frown
That I once couldn't see, oh silly me.

Rachael Batory (15)

HUNT

It's happening now I'm locked up in a rusty old cage.
Why me? What have I done?
With death at the tip of my claws,
I'm howling, thinking my family are gone.
My dad's been sold.
My mum's wrapped round her neck.
He's just doing it for the money.
That farmer should feel guilty
Us foxes haven't done anything, we're so innocent.
He's getting closer
Swishing through the grass his big black boots
With blood splattered on them.
With a click of that trigger I'll be gone forever.
Bang!
I'm not dead
It was the cage door,
He's set me free.

Laura O'Hanlon (12)

THE BRAVE DIE YOUNG

In that long and lonely trench line,
To which men come and go,
The soldier, brave and fearless,
I don't think he knows.

He doesn't know he's being used.
He's aware it's been two years.
He doesn't know how long it's going to be,
He was only a volunteer.

It was winter, 1918,
I went to visit Germany.
Here lies William John Smith,
Died for king and country.

Calum Bavin (14)

PIGGY BANK

Sitting or standing
Waiting for money

Looking fierce
Sweet and shy
Staying quiet
Never speaking
Never moving

Always listening
Time goes by
Empty, empty
Loads of time for getting fuller

Who? You ask
My piggy bank!

Megan Willmott (12)

LILLY

I have a flower called Lilly
Her petals are light and frilly,
She plays with her friends in the sun,
She's always having fun,
I love her ever so much,
I love the feel of her touch.
I don't like it when she goes,
When the wind huffs and puffs and blows,
But she'll come back again,
She'll dance with me in the rain.
She'll come with me to explore
And go right up to the shore.
She'll jump about wild and crazy,
But nothing like my neighbour's daisy.
She lives right next to the hutch,
Because she loves my bunny so much
And she loves me too,
She's never been so true.

Anaheta Sharifi (13)

SUMMER PANTOUM

Summer has finally surfaced
What a pleasant time for all
The bright colours in the sky
The warmth of the sun
What a pleasant time for all
The sound of children playing
The warmth of the sun
After the cold wait in winter
The sound of children playing
The bright colours in the sky
After the cold wait in winter
Summer has finally surfaced.

Tammy Samuel (15)

THE AXEMAN

With great satisfaction
The axeman plunges
His half ton axe into
Its lifeless body.
As he heaves and pulls,
His axe shines with its blood.

Next, he reaches for his saw.
Cutting off,
Limb by limb,
His mouth forms a glimmering smile
Filled with pleasure.
The axeman.
As he moves away
The forest of trees,
Is dead.

Megan Johnson (12)

QUESTIONS

I want to know, if you can tell me,
Why is the world so cruel?
Why can't we just live in peace
And let our communities rule?

Why do we have to send
Our troops away to fight
And let their poor families
Hope that they're alright?

And can you tell me why
The world is such a mess?
Why we hear about it every day
In the media and the press?

Why does all the bullying
Happen in the schools?
And at home; the workplace,
The bullies are the fools.

And answer this, if you can,
Why is there crime and violence?
Gangs of youths on the streets
Making everyone tense?

Why do I have all these questions,
About a world of hatred and war?
If you can't answer what I ask,
I still have explanations to look for.

Lucy Trafford (13)

DON'T STOP BELIEVING!

Don't stop believing
Keep chasing your dreams.
Don't give up hope.
Things will get worse before they get better.
It's not as hard as it seems.
So just keep chasing your dreams.
You can achieve anything if you truly believe!

Maddison Pryor (11)

JOY OF LIFE

I lay still on the grass,
The strange and dusty smell
Of cuttings flying through the breeze.

Inhale, exhale,
It comes naturally to me.
I rest there listening to the song of the birds,
Leaves rustle on the trees,
The excited screams of children in the distance.

I could lay there for hours
Listening to the life surrounding us.
Life, what a beautiful creation,
It astounds me,
It's amazing and incredible.

We can open our eyes every day
Conscious that we're alive.

Tabitha Emily Bridges (15)

LIFE'S NIGHT

Red nails clutched the death wish,
Smoke ventured from her lips,
For she could hardly see good,
Instead saw fog before the ships.

Sprawled along the rocks,
Words lay unfinished on her hands,
Thoughts hung like lace around her mind,
Like cobwebs on books from other lands.

Borrowed time leaves old and young,
Pictures, memories, silver and gold,
Slipping away, a slow vertigo,
Rung on the rusty bells of souls old.

Sweeping, swiftly into the night,
Pulling her hood to cloud her face,
She knows what's left of the world,
That each life is only a race.

Faaria Khan (15)

THE MAN THAT WASN'T THERE!

You're the sinister shadow casting off the window sill.
You're the evil snare in a drug dealer's pill.
You're the hand reaching out pretending that you care.
I wouldn't touch it,
No I wouldn't dare!
Disfigured head without a face,
People's features you like to displace.
People's blood you like to taste.
You woo your victims with a seductive tone.
Your voice whispering like a sickly drone,
But I know you have a more insidious agenda.
Please leave me alone . . . I surrender!
I know that you're after me,
Tell me why do you find so much glee
In killing people so ruthlessly?
You laugh at me in mocking tone,
Oh no here it comes that sickly sweet drone!
Oh stop it, stop it, he doesn't really care,
But it was too late,
I was already in his lair.
And then I knew . . .
I was going to be devoured by the man that wasn't there.

Rhian Pearce (15)

THE STUFF THAT GETS CAUGHT IN OUR TEACHER'S BEARD!

The stuff that's all sticky and slimy,
The stuff that's all green and weird,
The stuff that gets caught in our teacher's beard.

The spaghetti that always misses his mouth,
If I fed it him back I doubt he would eat it,
Or maybe just a tiny-weeny little bit.

So watch out for your teacher's beard,
You might get *your* face all yucky and weird!

Charlotte Harvey (8)

HE BEAUTY OF A SMILE

A smile is an infectious, precious and priceless gift that you can treasure,
It is worth more than gold.
A smile costs nothing, it is free,
A smile can spread from you to me.
A smile is precious, gentle and unique
And it can travel around the world in one language.
A smile shines bright like a ray of sunshine,
A smile appears when you're having fun.
It shines all around because it's not just mine,
You don't have to go and get a sensational smile,
Because it can travel over a mile.
A smile can break through a frown
And can travel all over the town.
Rich or poor everyone can be enriched with a smile,
A smile can change your emotions in a quick motion.
A smile may look like a little thing yet it can make a big difference,
You can't steal, borrow or break it because it is strong.
A smile gains more power every hour,
A smile can appear anywhere.
It is a free flow which can lift you up when you are feeling low.
This the stunning beauty of a smile.

Kaliyah-Destiny Sesay (9)

SPRING COMES AND GOES

I remember when I was at the park
It was spring day!
All the flowers were bloomed
From roses and violets
To lilacs and daffodils.
Ducks quacking as loud as they can.
The breeze blowing in my face to keep me cool.
The water was so transparent that I could see my face.
As the sun set the mountains started
To make a wonderful shade of grey.
The trees started to dance to the
Wonderful lullaby sung by the blackbirds.
That's all I can remember, there's not a thing I missed out!
Summer comes next but not till later.

Danielle Maseko (10)

THE GREY WOODLAND WOLF

Like the grey woodland wolf
who howls to the moon
A voice so loud but words unheard
He screams out his soul
A confession to a closed door
of a beloved spirit's concern

I'm reaching out a hand trying hard
no one's path is straight and set
obstacles lie ahead in life
Why can't he see
that no one runs easily?
We all stumble and trip
but we get back up on our feet

Like the grey woodland wolf
who adores that moon
Silver and bright, she glows
Nothing but perfect
One of a kind, the full moon shines
An amazing thing
She's still loved as she's admired
Alone at night, essence alike
Silver and bright, she glows
Talents glow alight

How can she be so blind
and continue to live without living?
What sort of life is that?

Like the grey woodland wolf
and the brightest moon
Dreams a shade only they can see
fade as dawn evades
The light paints the brightest of skies
It hides the shades no one will see
Only alone the fragrance shows
So wait till the hour
of the grey woodland wolf.

Shelby Wade-Gudgin (16)

THE VAMPIRE WITH A SOUL!

They're hidden in the night,
They're never seen in light,
You're taken by the fright.
Then they take a lethal bite.

Your streaming blood is thin,
Under a layer of skin
And that's when it begins.

Low your body hangs,
As I retract my fangs,
With them you skin I pierce
And blood pumps out so fierce.

'We'll kill them with a stake,
C'mon it'll be a piece of cake,
They're killing the whole town,
They cannot stick around.'

Her blood is so revealing,
I can't resist the feeling,
The sensation is so appealing,
My hunger is now healing.

I've taken too much,
I've given into lust,
I have to stop, I must.

I'm killing her I know,
They're coming I must go,
They will kill me for sure,
I've got to find a cure.

'We'll kill them with a stake,
C'mon it'll be a piece of cake,
He's killing my daughter now,
He cannot stick around.'

I am fed,
She's almost dead,
She should be in a hospital bed,
But her blood is still pouring out red.

She must be saved,
In her blood she is bathed,
For feeding on her I am shamed.

I love her too much,
To be without her touch,
It's killing me inside,
She must stay *alive!*

Jade Lam (13)

THE WORLD IS WEEPING

I stopped in my haste to look at our world today.
All the smiling faces had long gone.
I heard my mother say
There is no love from the children of today.
They walk around like they are depressed
And old in their young hallowed shells.
I sit wrapped in vines, my eyes a withered rose.
These thorns have stabbed into my heart and made it cold.
I dreamt that there was light again
And my saviour came and said he'd protect me from the end.
My mother woke up, she said I wept,
I still ache for those days unkept.
I fly down rainbows and I see dead men
And I stop the cold from coming in.
I stop in my haste to look at what they have done to our world today.
As they say there is no more love these days.

Zinat Khatun (16)

TAKE OFF YOUR COLOURS

Take these colours that we wear to blend in with the rest,
These protective coats of normality, convinced we must impress.

Take these colours that we wear and throw them to the floor,
Show that individuality has a strength we can't ignore.

Now join me friends to shed these coats, the caves in which we hide.
Shed your colours to show the world who you are inside.

Rebecca Meredith (16)

MORE THAN A DREAM . . .

Last night I dreamt of sorrow,
In a forest of shadows.
There was not a speck of light,
But there was a distant candle.

I walked towards the light,
But I was trapped by a vine,
I stepped through the terror,
So I could get closer to the shine.

I felt the warm tingle,
It was filling my heart up,
Suddenly I fell through a hole,
I landed with a *thump!*

Everything was bright red,
It had faces of anger,
I ran and ran into a dragon,
It rose and I climbed on her.

The dragon soared into the air,
I heard the blue sky weeping,
Tears were falling from the clouds,
Then the dragon got sleepy.

I tried to keep her head straight,
But her body just vanished,
I fell down, down, down,
I fell into a mist.

I had crystal white wings,
They carried me to a blur,
I saw my friends and family,
Was this a place of love?

My feet touched the ground,
I could see the light once more,
I shut my eyes and charged forward,
I will get to it for sure!

My eyes opened wide,
I was resting in my bed,
This can't have been just a dream,
As there was a feather on my head.

Thasin Choudhury (13)

LIFE IN A BUBBLE

This little bubble we live in
Has become our perfect world:
Our fantasies seem to be reality:
Our hopes become our expectations.

We hate to love it
And we love to hate it,
Yet it becomes painful
To leave this bubble.

We stand at the edges,
Looking out into the real world,
Saying we want to be part of it,
Not quite ready to step forward.

We know it will happen:
One day this safe bubble
Will disappear around us
As we stand rooted in shock.

Then reality will deafen us
As it comes rushing at us,
Until we find another bubble
To safely reside in.

But as we are now,
In our current bubble,
Reality seeps through its skin,
Reminding us of what awaits.

Each and every one of us,
In our own little bubbles,
Those transparent cocoons,
Live in separate worlds.

We look outwards
Through distorting walls,
Dreaming of life elsewhere
In another bubble.

When our bubble
Overlaps with another's,
We catch a rare glimpse
Of someone else's world.

As we float through life
In our little bubble,
Remember that for each person
There is their own world.

Arani Navaneethakrishnan (17)

SUMMER PARK

The swings gently sway,
carried by the breeze.
Cherry blossom covers,
the gorgeous majestic trees.

There isn't a cotton cloud,
in the azure sky.
The birds are singing a beautiful song,
and no one wonders why.

There is a honey coloured cottage,
perched on the luscious hill.
There is the sound of running water,
coming from the mill.

And as the evening draws closer,
the light begins to fade.
The people start gathering their bags,
and heading towards the gate . . .

Kate Hall (9)

THE CHILD

The discreet stranger walking through the streets
not a shoe nor a sandal upon his feet
fear and sorrow confine his darkened face
with him he carries a photo and a frame

tears fall down his soft cheek
his face tired and his body weak
his torn clothes and broken heart
carry him further but tear him apart

his pain and feelings sentimental
his silent footsteps soft and gentle
he walks through the deserted streets
with nothing in aid but, his swollen feet.

Sara Asif (14)

THE UNICORN

A mane of truth
And hooves of gold -
Where the unicorn roams,
No lies are told.
She lights up the sky,
Bringing new life
Breaking open the void;
Horn sharp as a knife.
Eyes blue as sea,
The angels her friends,
A love broken heart
The unicorn mends.
Singing songs of no tune
She lets all the world know,
That no one's to hide
And soft is *no* blow.
So as she sits in the glade
And wishes world true,
No person shall suffer -
No person like you.

Bethany Nelson (13)

SLEEP TIGHT!

(Inspired by Remembrance Day)

Out there he fights with a single gun,
I do not think he's having fun!

While I lay in bed and cry in sorrow,
My big brave daddy won't come home tomorrow.

I wear a red poppy on my right,
I know he's passed out of the light!

I say *thank you* for giving your life tonight,
I pray for you Daddy, sleep tight!

Bethany Wilson (10)

THE HOUSE THAT WAS

The clock had stopped,
His hand is still,
The wintry wind is calm.
The sad little floorboards,
Creak to their mother,
The electricity clicks off.

Upstairs the paper peels,
Acting sorry for itself indeed,
The fireplace is empty, cold as it could be.
The large bedroom seems so small,
Its windows crying with dust,
The wooden wardrobe in the corner shouting out for love.

But still I love this broken house
And its odd but wonderful charms.
The memories as fresh as yesterday,
Coming back with every glance.
But I turn my head, and run for the car,
As my house will, be remembered.

Charlotte Leigh Edgar (14)

DEAD ROTTING PILE

As she straggled her broken body across the cracked floor,
Her bony fingers creaked as she reached for the door.
'Speak to me,' she echoed round the room,
'Or you never know I might be back soon.'

A few years later in that old dusty house,
Everything silent not even a mouse.
You hear her bones dragged along the floor
And out pops her head from the side of the door.

She comes to the room as she creaks and groans,
Up she gets with a long, loud moan.
She stands up on her feet and walks for a while,
But then she is just a dead rotting pile.

Emily Rose Whitworth (12)

ONE SUMMER'S DAY

I lay in the garden with nothing to do,
Nothing old and nothing new!
So I went to my gran's house,
Where I saw a small brown mouse.
I yelled and screamed
And Gran's cat beamed.
They chased and chased
And I learnt to paste.
It was my gran that showed me how
Which is something my mom would never allow.
I read all my books
And I looked at some of Grandad's fishing hooks
Then I was bored again,
So some knowledge I tried to gain
I even read the dictionary
And played a game of Pictionary!
I swear my gran let me win
But I did put her glasses in the bin!
In the end I wrote a beautiful story
About a fair maiden in all her golden glory.
She met a handsome prince
Who managed to convince
The lovely maiden to fall in love
Around the most beautiful silver white dove.
I wrote and wrote until the sun went down
When the golden princess wore the crown.
I went home and straight to bed
After, of course, being fed!
It turned out I had the best day ever
I don't want the holidays to stop, never, never, *never!*

Sophie Rose Ryan-Marrison (12)

MORTALITY

Why there's nothing
so majestic, so stupendous and strong
as
the human body. So
perfected in its intricacies
that one simple sneeze can
completely corrupt its complexities.
Where the cells have more
freedom than the people.
They decide upon mutinous mutations
beyond all control.

Our design is our demise.

They sit complacently
eyes glazed and glaring over
scarlet nose and sallow skin,
united only in conviction that their illness is
the worst.

They knock. With their
filthy fingers, and prepare their
monologue.
Pathetic sickly whining
act as if they're dying.

How the callous and cold-hearted
fall to their knees
vying
for my sympathy.
Oh, don't they know,
the wrong pill could kill?
Would seem such an innocent
mistake;
not been sleeping - another ache
nothing more to contemplate.

Young so stupid - old still foolish
'I won't eat I'm gonna drink I'm gonna sniff
some powdered random debris
test my body till
the bitter end.'
And every
time, they're in the clear
but not
me, I'm

terminal.
It's

C-a-n-c-e-r
Ca-ca-can . . . can-cer . . .
Every single empty day
I have to say
it, to someone, so why   can't I
say it, even whisper
it, to myself?

I'm their God; they want - demand - a
miracle cure,
I can fix them but
not their real problem

inside.

But oh sweet, merciful God, who
scorns me, mocks me,
laughs at me, laughs,
gives me the power
tingling
in my fingertips, over
life and death yet
not

my own.

Hannah Dickinson (16)

IT'S AMAZING

It's amazing when I look up,
The stars shine and moon glistens,
Then the wind whispers softly in your ears,
'Everything's as it should be.'

It's amazing when I sit in silence,
The voice of the world gently hums,
The colours of this life dance in harmony
And I think things couldn't be better.

It's amazing when I lay in bed,
The darkness surrounding me,
The warmth embracing me,
And life is taking steady breaths.

This thing called life,
It's amazing.

Zita Gordon (16)

BE STRONG

When the north winds blow
You know it's time to go.
A cloud forms in the sky
Ready to lift you way up high.
Be strong.
The doctors tried in vain
To free you from your pain,
To make you live again
To save you from that train.
Be strong
Now you are a ghost,
I still love you the most.
I sent up a balloon,
When I look up at the moon,
I see your face and smile
Though I won't see you for a while.
When I saw you I said hi,
But now I have to say goodbye.
Be strong.

Jade Haughton (12)

SKIN-DEEP

People believe they can condense beauty
Into a sweet smelling liquid,
Or a cleansing balm.
But would the finest of roses
Be any more beautiful
If it was given a new face and smell?

Beauty cannot be held in a crystal bottle,
It does not dwell in plastic jars,
Rather, it lies beneath the surface
Pure and without excess.
It lies in the heart,
And shines like sunlight,
Illuminating perfection within imperfection
And love gives us new eyes
So that we may see it.
Even if not all behold it,
It is there for one to see
And be left in awe.

Because this beauty is never just skin deep.

Jonathan Foard (17)

HENRY'S SONG

I will go on an adventure -
I will go on a quest -
So keep in mind my destiny -
Don't worry about the distance -
Don't care about the time.

Henry Fandey (9)

SURELY

Surely, if it happened today,
That boys left home too early,
And marched away in shiny black boots,
Someone amongst the crowd would shout,
'They're going to die! Don't send them away.'

Surely, if it happened today,
That thick russet mud was the ground,
And darkness grabbed men in trenches
Someone would help save their tired feet
From the lice, trench foot, the rotting and decay.

Surely, if it happened today,
That men half dead were flung into trees,
And those left alive were screaming,
Someone would let them return home,
And put an end to the most hell-ridden fray.

Surely, if it happened today,
That an old man of twenty-eight years,
Limped home, fear bold in his eyes,
Someone would ask what had happened,
And question with doubt, why the young had to pay.

Surely, if they had known,
That graveyards would be so full of youth
And women would grow old alone,
Someone would have stopped and realised
That their country's pride is nothing compared to lives.

Sophie Foreman (15)

LIFE IS A CHESS GAME

You are all judges of each other,
For you inherit the prejudices from your fathers and mothers.
You are influenced by the authorities of your time
And continue to defy your virtues, for the guilty pleasures are sublime.
Smoking, drinking, drugs and money are your vices,
In which you devour in excess if the cost suffices.
Whether that cost be pain on another victim's life,
It doesn't matter for religion will always offer the afterlife.
You have your countries; you have your land,
But your greed is not happy and wants to expand.
You have the opponents' citizens' lives in your hands, what does your enemy have?
Nothing but the punishment of remand.
You want all the wonders that the universe can submit to you,
Which you can have if you take that bite from the apple tree.
Can you guess who I am? I'm responsible for all,
Humankind's failures in which they stretch further than the Chinese wall.
I am Lucifer, known as the Devil, the fallen angel if you like,
You are God's chess pieces, wallowing in the delight.
Soon to be taken by my skillful hand,
Not to be given choices that's just too bland.
I'm offering you the afterlife, the eternal existence,
But at the price of your choices, God shall I say has acted on passive resistance.
Which I can overcome with violence which he knows too well,
But you have sinned and so you are damned in Hell.

Broch Anglestone (16)

NOBODY'S PERFECT

Why do people hate being themselves?
They have got to face that everyone's unique
No one can change who we are or what we are
Who cares if you're a geek or even a popular freak?

Some are disabled, some are not and some are short and some are not
Face it, we're all not the same!
Some have curly hair, some have straight
Laughing for being different is just so lame!

At the end of the day,
Just look at yourself in the mirror and you will see,
A beautiful person standing in front of you
Be happy and say out loud with confidence, 'That's me!'

Why do people hate others who are different?
Yes, we may be different on the outside
But we are as alike as two peas in a pod on the inside
Let being yourself fill your heart with pride.

Why hate yourself when you are sure,
That you are not alone in knowing that nobody's perfect!

Mathusha Manokaran (13)

ON STAGE

Lights blaring down,
Music from the dark pit below rises and swells,
The audience are waiting,
Their breath held for the next surprise in store.
The lavish sets rise and fall around me,
I see twirling satins and spinning silks of the dancing ensemble.
This is my big moment,
The beginning of my life . . . on stage.

Beth Younge (17)

SUMMER HOLIDAYS

(Dedicated to Alantica Sun Gardens Hotel, Cyprus)

Blue, green and dark blue
Beautiful and clear all the way through
Shipwrecks are hard to find
Amazing marine life one of a kind
Dazzling coral takes the stage
Exploring is fun whatever the age
Sunshine all the way
Sea, sand and sun make the day
Up above a dip in the pool
You have got to admit this is cool
Drink from the bar
Relax in the spa
This is what holidays are for . . .
Sun, relax and no school.

Summer holidays.

Charlotte Prestwich (11)

DISCO DIVA

I am a disco diva
I have a groovy fever
I dance wherever I go
So come and book me for a show
I dance like Michael Jackson
I do a lot of crazy action
My body is unstoppable
That's why I'm a professional

The music I like is funky
I am a little monkey
I have pure music fashion
I have pure music passion
I have a tremendous balance
As well as lots of other talents
If you ever get to see me
You'll be very, very lucky
I am a disco diva
I have a groovy fever.

Evie Richards (11)

I LIVE MY LIFE!

I live, I breathe, I dream.
My dreams speak of tranquillity.
A sea of equality and tolerance is left emulsified in a quilt;
A quilt of materialism and malevolence.
In time, some time, that sea will flow as elegantly as the silk unfolding from the weaver's roll.
Until that change in our world happens,
Our generation of racism and violence belongs, in truth.
I speak, I move, I believe,
I believe in what I want.
People judge others by what they wear.
What they say.
By looks.
Their beliefs.
In a perfect world, everyone will have a choice.
A choice to life.
Everyone will be equal.
Friends will be friends because of personalities and not looks.
Fights and arguments will be found only in innocent children's nightmares
And not on the drunken streets and alleys
Or in the public houses from the villages and valleys,
But that perfect world will only ever be, a perfect dream.
I play, I love, I think.
My thoughts are the key to my life.
The golden, rigid key.
Sometimes the key goes rusty and is forgotten;
But my thoughts can't and won't be locked away by any key - by anyone!
At any time.
Any place.
For any reason.
I am who I am because of the things I think.
If I ever see a shooting star,
Rapidly racing through the opaque night sky,
I will make an amicable wish.
A wish that everyone, everywhere could express their thoughts and feelings.
That everyone could be respected for who they truly are
And what they think.
I live, I breathe, I dream a tranquil dream.

Beth Buchanan (13)

MEMORIES

As I sit here now thinking back,
How many friends I lost, how many friends didn't grow old - like me.
It seems like only yesterday,
How quickly these 65 years have flown by,
If I close my eyes. I am there again.

I can hear the sound of deafening gunfire rattling
And the many bombs exploding all around me.
The screams of young men,
Just boys really who had never seen war before
And who wouldn't see home again.
The smells of gunpowder, fresh blood and disturbed dirt.

As I look around I see soldiers, some my friends, crying, being shot,
Mud and blood flying and bullets whizzing past.
I crouch down, frightened for my life,
I dodge bullets and cry as quietly as I can into my hands.
Then suddenly, pain strikes me like nothing I had ever felt before.
It takes my breath away and as I look down,
A hole has been shot right trough my upper leg
And blood is staining my trousers,
A brilliant red colour, it spits angrily out at me.
The pain keeps on coming as I stared, not knowing what to do.
I couldn't speak couldn't move and then blackness covers me like a blanket.

I open my eyes - back again, alone in the busy day room,
I try to catch my breath quietly, not wanting to be noticed.
I look down and see my one and only leg, the other gone many years ago,
Just like my friends - gone forever.
All I have to keep me company are my memories of lost friends
And heroes of my youth.

James Gordon (10)

THE BATTLE OF HASTINGS

This poem is about the Battle of Hastings
Nearly a thousand years ago
A cruel, brutal, medieval time
As most of you will know.

So, shortly after King Edward died,
Harold became the royal king
But William of Normandy kicked up a fuss
And said, 'I should be the one that's ruling!'

William took this as an excuse to start war
He wanted to start up a fight
Because William was a very selfish man
And he thought being king was his right!

William sailed over to England with his army
He looked brave but he was full of fright
Because he knew that once he landed on shore
The battle would be on within a night!

Meanwhile Harold was far up north
And had heard nothing about the intrusion
But when he heard that William had landed
He sailed south with his soldiers in confusion.

He met Duke William on Senlac Hill
His soldiers brave and strong
But, what Harold didn't know
Was that the Normans had a plan all along.

They battled for around 10 hours
The English falling all around
Then the Norman soldiers turned and ran away
While Duke William lay face down.

The English realised what had happened quite quick
They ran after the Normans with cheer
But then William stood up, and with a triumphant grin
He said, 'My knights! Come back here!'

The Normans turned around on their horses
Their helmets balanced well on their heads
They pulled the strings on their bows
And shot all the English dead.

One arrow was shot with perfect aim
It went right up into the sky
Then it came shooting down, at the speed of light
And shot King Harold in the eye.

From that moment on William was the king
The ruler of the remaining Saxons
And not once in his life, not ever, ever, ever
Did he feel sorry for his actions.

And that was the end of the Battle of Hastings
Our tale has come to an end
But don't be sad, as you will hear it again
Through generations, this tale will descend.

Sacha Beswick (12)

THE HEROIN

I am your heroin
But not your average, everyday heroin,
Do I wail and cry for help, locked in the tallest tower?
No, rather I cause the wailing, the silent cries for help,
While locking my victims in their broken minds.
Is there a prince to save me, to grant me my happy ending?
No, there is only the addiction to me,
I am your saviour for a few hours, then your destroyer for a lifetime.
There is no happy ending, there is just me, your salvation in this world that I painted black.
You cling to me, I who am the sole cause of your ruin.
Your devastation and soulless cries; my sweet melody and comfort.
Evil witches and stepmothers have nothing on me.
If all those years ago you had resisted temptation,
My dark curse might not have been cast.

But you are the one who chose me.
You are the one who smokes me, draws me in.
You are the one who can't live without me.
You are the one who has forsaken yourself.
We will go side by side as I drag you into the black flame of death.
I stayed with you forever but you were forever alone.
You didn't save me, I couldn't save you.
Only you could have saved yourself.
But I am heroin.

Maryam Adil (14)

SUMMER IS . . .

Summer is melting ice lollies,
Summer is golden sand between your toes,
Summer is the sea crashing against your body,
Summer is flowers opening to show you their smiling faces,
Summer is BBQs and party music,
Summer is a season you can never forget!

Zoë Lane (14)

BROKEN AND EMPTY

Life throws the most degrading things,
How could he do that yet like an angel he sings?
I've never felt so used,
Never felt so hurt and confused.

I still don't understand,
This odd and crazy land,
But you are the biggest mystery of all,
How can you say all that and then sit back and watch me fall?

I thought you cared but I guess I was wrong.
I remember how my smile grew when I heard our song,
Now it means nothing, just a painful memory.
I didn't know at the time this love was only temporary.

I'm sick of crying, I've done it too much,
But my heart remains within your clutch,
The ache in my chest has dulled down,
However on my face I still wear a frown.

I'll say this once, and once only
I truly mean it when I say you ruined me . . .

Emma Newell (13)

SUMMER

Summer is my favourite season of the year.
The sun comes out and there's a fresh scent in the air.
No school means freedom is here,
Walking to the park I can hear the children cheer.
They're having fun with ice cream in their hands,
While mums and dads are chilling in the sand.
Frisbees fill the air and balls flying everywhere,
Skipping ropes, bikes and teddy bears,
That's why summer is my favourite season of the year.

Muhibur Rahman (10)

THE GARDEN OF EDEN

The Garden of Eden is a wonderful place,
some of the animals you may recognise by face.
There are two eye-catching rainbows sailing over the mountains,
there is aqua blue water trickling down the fountains.
There is emerald green grass, which no one can trespass.
The sun beams shine bright, showing off a lot of light.
The Garden of Eden is the start of creation.

The Garden of Eden is a beautiful patch,
there's a man and a woman that make a perfect match.
Of course their names are Adam and Eve,
they are kind and honest I believe.
The animals are as colourful as can be,
the fast flowing falls are a sight you must see.
The mighty mountains reach up to the sky,
where the rainbow butterflies flutter by.
The Garden of Eden is our fantastic life.

Heather Hyde (9)

THE MIND OF A CHOCOHOLIC

Creamy and white, or rich and deep brown,
Such a nice taste, you can't help but smile.
Melted on strawberries or mixed into cake,
Gooey and sticky, too good to be true.

Oozing and flowing, over the fountain,
Delicate and refined, as truffle in a shell.
Mixed up with milk, so hot and steaming,
Or poured on as icing, I don't really mind.

Swirling and swimming in a chocolate sea,
Smooth and warm qualities all around me.
Seeps into my mouth and tastes oh so good,
My heart yearns for more but I can't get enough.

Oozing and flowing, over the fountain,
Delicate and refined, as truffle in a shell.
Mixed up with milk, so hot and steaming,
Or poured on as icing, any will do!

Rachel Attwood (14)

KNIFE CRIME

Knife crime is a problem,
Wherever you may go.
People think knives help them
And it's not just youths you know.

It could be an adult,
Or a gang or a yob.
It could happen after an insult,
Or you could be trying to rob.

It could just be for safety,
Or to harm, if you're under the weather.
But remember this reality,
Carrying a knife don't make you clever.

It doesn't make you strong,
When you take it out your house,
Carrying a knife is wrong
And if you've got one, you're the mouse.

So when you're seeing red
And you reach out for the knife.
Just keep thinking in your head,
It could take away a life.

Craig Fahey (15)

A DAY WITH THE FAMILY

Can you hear the whisper blowing in the breeze?
Can you feel the coldness of the winter freeze?
Can you see the colours of the smiling sun?
Can you hear the children playing and having fun?
Can you feel the happiness floating in the air?
A day with the family really seems fair!

Tara Lawless (14)

THE SUN

I am a sun, have some tea and a bun,
As you watch me shine, on that vine.
Look at me,
I can glisten on that tree . . .
But don't shine on that bee . . .
I can glow, but very slow,
And I'm telling you, when I'm around, don't wear a bow.
I am yellow, but please don't bellow.
It will deafen me.
Oh! There's that bee, coming to sting me!

There's a hot-air balloon!
Hey! Hot-air balloon, see you soon.
Just a second, it's David Beckham!
Here we are chatting,
Oh! There's a man batting!

You're being very nice.
I have some cake . . . have a slice.
Yes I know, I'm a sun,
And you've just had a bun.
But have a treat.
Oh no! It's raining sleet.
Oh, then, goodbye, you really are sly.
I'll be back soon, with my hot-air balloon.

Here I am again
Now there's no rain.
It's such a pain, when it rains.
Hey rain, don't do it again.

There you are friend, I found you at last.
We had a good time in the past.
I am the sun.
Remember me?
When I nearly got stung by a bee?

Yes, you do. Me too.
Now let's go to the pool, where it's nice and cool.

I'll shine down on you.
I don't take any interest in vines now.
I can shine
On your little pine . . . cone.

Tee hee! There's the bee.
How on earth did he find me?
Wait a minute, it's after you.
Hey you bee, get off my friend,
Or she will bend.

Are you alright?
Oh no, you're stung
And just because you are so young.

Have this stuff, it will kill the pain.
Hooray! You are alright again!
What shall we do?
Just for you?
Yes, I mean you,
Because you were nice to me.

Hannah Shorrock (7)

A CINDERELLA STORY

You may not think this story is swell,
but kiss that traditional tale goodbye, farewell.
Because this is my version that I have done,
now listen as my story's begun.
It was just another day,
well it was for Cinderella anyway.
Sweeping, dusting, cleaning the fire,
all that she had was hope and desire.
But that's of course why they called her Cinders,
she always had fire ash under her fingers.
She had used all her hopes and wishes,
she was tired of washing all the dishes.
Her real name was Cinderella,
her two ugly stepsisters said she wouldn't find a fella.
They always, always had to boast,
especially when their invite came in the post.
On the night Cinders was at home alone,
with nothing to do, not even a mobile phone.
Until out of the blue,
her biggest dream came true.
With a bisch and a boosh,
and a wish and a whoosh.
As a lady appeared in a cloud of pink,
Cinders had time to stop and think.
Because she was confused inside,
who was this lady, should she run and hide?
She was standing there in a dress of white,
she was a big lady, so it was quite tight!
She told Cinders she meant no harm,
she normally inspires people with her constant charm.
I will cast you one wish, with this wand in my hand,
because for now this wish is my command.
I'm your fairy godmother, go ahead and take a look,
through this massive spell book.
Pick from these, choose from them all,
but all Cinders wanted was to go to the ball.
So as her fairy godmother had promised, Cinders wish came true,
she was standing at the door in a dress of sparkly blue.
Two glass slippers upon her feet,
at least it was night, so they wouldn't smell in the heat!
She turned a pumpkin into a carriage,
fit for a princess at a royal marriage.
Two rats into horses of white,

their sparkling fur reflecting in the moonlight.
Everything was ready just one thing left to say,
this wasn't a silly game to play.
Fairy godmother said she must be home for midnight,
or she would have a terrible fright.
But off she went,
without actually knowing what she'd meant.
But never mind that, what if her name wasn't on the list?
What if it was another stupid fairy tale with an awkward twist?
Cinders walked into the ball and caught the prince's eye,
he watched her sit on a chair nearby.
He walked over and took her by the hand,
asking her to dance in front of the live classical band.
She obviously agreed and at once got to her feet,
she danced gracefully with him all night, stepping to the beat.
Finally the clock struck midnight,
Cinders ran out of the room at the speed of light.
Leaving one's slipper accidentally behind,
for her Prince Charming to eventually find.
So the search began, every day and every night,
the prince wasn't going to give up without a fight.
He searched for many a day,
until his hope started to die down and go away.
Rat-a-tat-tat,
who was that?
The two ugly sisters opened the door,
the prince was scared at what he saw.
But still he walked in,
with a convincing grin.
The two sisters fought to see who would try first,
but one was too big and the other just wouldn't fit.
Now it was Cinders' turn to try on the show,
the sisters argued a bit, but they eventually came through.
Cinders tried it on, it was of course a perfect fit,
the prince's grin grew bigger, enough to stretch from armpit to armpit.
Her two stepsisters' mouths dropped, their minds a blank,
as both of their hearts totally sank.
Of course they were married,
and into the sunset they were carried.
No more dishes for Cinders to clean,
no more ugly stepsisters being mean.
Because all of her dreams had now come true,
no more feeling down or blue.

All that she needs is right through the palace door,
why wish, when there's nothing to wish for.
I know these stories get dafter and dafter,
but I have to end with the original . . . they lived happily ever after!

Hollie Terrell (12)

LIFE OF AN IMMIGRANT

It all begins with the joy of entering a new country
The excitement of being reunited with family
The happiness of building a better future for the children
Counting every possibility that may lead to success
The feeling that makes you think everything's going to be okay.

Everything changes once you've outstayed your visit
Family soon become foe
Everything feels much harder
Stress and depression then takes its toll
The struggle to build a future for your children
You can't even see the path ahead

But there is sunshine after the storm
When you finally have the right to remain in the country
The fight was worth fighting for
The feeling of accomplishment
You made it!
Life finally feels perfect at last.

Atia Joynob (13)

LIFE TO ME

Life is everywhere
It is on you and forever it shall stay.
Life is the wind blowing sideways.
Life is the winter and the summer.
I am life, you are life, we are life.
Life and I play beneath the morning sun.
Life and I play beneath the midnight moon.
Life brings me soup when I am ill.
Life kisses me goodnight and greets me with a smile.
Life is sad and it is lonely.
Life is evil and life is blunt.
Life is a true friend and never lies.
I am life, you are life, we are life.

Lydia Adebajo (14)

I LOVE YOU

I'm sorry but I don't know who you are
I'm sorry that I don't know your name
I'm sorry but I don't know what you are
You're like a stranger to me
I'm sorry but I can't remember the sound of your voice
I'm sorry I don't remember your face
I'm sorry I don't remember the colour of your eyes
Or the colour of your hair
I'm sorry I don't remember anything
But why did you leave me
Why did you have to go?
Without a warning, you were gone
I hate you is what I should say
But that would all be a lie.

I love you, even though you're a stranger
I love you, even though I don't know your name
I love you because I know you're watching me
You're always protecting me when I'm vulnerable
You're always there, trying to make me happy
And I know even though I'm in a different world
I know you're still watching over me
Like my guardian angel in the heavens
Even though we're strangers
We know everything about nothing about each other
Even though we never really met.

Christine Nyambura Murimi (14)

HOME

Tiny shoots of flowers begin to show,
Bright yellow petals breaking up the snow.
The snow and ice have finally stopped,
The farmer starts to plant his crops.

When spring hits the hills
So do excitement and thrills.
The lambs begin to appear,
All the little calls you hear.

Our Eisteddfod comes in summertime,
Nobody hears the clock chime.
Pwllheli beach stretches afar,
We stay so late out come the stars.

Cracks of thunder shake through the valley,
On our way home we do not dally.
Hoping the signal is still there,
Dad on the roof trying to repair.

Watching Eve Myles, she's back on set,
Dad's still up there getting wet.

As Snowdon starts to lose its peak,
Down come the heavy snow and sleet.
Conway Castle covered in a blanket of white,
Yet it is still the most amazing sight.

Down to Cardiff Bay we head,
We didn't even go to bed.

The Christmas lights are said to be bright,
Red, green and white lighting up the night.

A dragon dominates our great flag,
But no it's not a tiny rag.

When the farmer brings in the big hay bales,
This is the best place to be on Earth . . . Wales!

Portia-Hope Kitney (14)

THE WORD

The future vision, ripped from all things true.
Too blind, too hurt, too foolish in facing.
From hurt eyes can only see me as I said.
'Tis not hope, 'tis not fear,
'Tis greater than all who can see it.
Can they see through a mask of sorrow?
Do they look . . . can they sense? Do they care?
Not does anything mask my questions,
Because they cannot be answered.
Only by feeling can any see.
A feeling that does not wish to
But knows what the only reason is.
Hurt hidden, lost, found,
From down here none see me.
For I want nothing if they are too hurt to talk.
It is because she knows no bounds,
Nothing stops her saying what is not yet hers to tell.
A mask with no constancy.
A shell with no inside.
Heartless that's the word.

Charlotte Whellams (15)

WHEN WORLDS COLLIDE

Whispers of the past, carried by the winds of change.
Lilting melodies that caress the golden fringes of reality.
When worlds collide.
The vicious cycle of life and death, the hunter and the hunted.
Fields of flowers hide the decay of lives under layers of dirt.
When worlds collide.
Water clashes with land as the ocean takes back what is hers.
The majestic beauty of the sun, as it scorches the land, starves the innocent.
When worlds collide.
The blissful memories die with age, the pages of the past lie untouched.
Hearts fester and blacken, feelings are forgotten.
When worlds collide.
The beauty of the blade, silent and deadly.
The souls scattered amongst the stars, the dreams dissolved amidst tears.
When worlds collide.

Qesma Mohammed (17)

A NAME POEM

A is for Albert who breaks his toys
B is for Berty who runs after boys
C is for Corey who drives a lorry
D is for Dylan who never says sorry
E is for Eric who wants five cars
F is for Fred who eats chocolate bars
G is for Greg who scares cows
H is for Harold who shoots arrows and bows
I is for Ian who has three cats
J is for Jack who likes to buy mats
K is for Kevin who likes rockets
L is for Lucy who has baggy pockets
M is for Milo who has a plastic bun
N is for Norris who watches the setting sun
O is for Olly who likes toys that are fake
P is for Polly who eats chocolate cake
Q is for Quack who lives in a pond
R is for Ronald who watches James Bond
S is for Sally who likes Spider-Man
T is for Tracey who has a tin can.

Benyamin Juma (9)

WHAT IS LOVE?

Love is family, friends, the perfect guy,
The first kiss on Valentine's evening.
Love is more precious than money can buy,
Someone who's reliable and caring:
They don't care what you look like or how you
Act; they'll love you for who you truly are.
The people who'll do lots to help you,
From work and money to driving a car.
Love is found in unexpected places:
A white knight behind the glasses and books,
The fair princess in the gaudy braces,
Beauty is unearthed if one really looks.
Love is the good times and bad times combined,
Trust in each other and love you shall find.

Beatrice Anderson (13)

THE WATERBORNE TRAVELLERS

They stand with solemn hearts and hopeful eyes as they descend into the beginning
They leave behind those people, those memories and those fears
But as they clamber into the boat their porcelain shells shiver and smash
All that is left is the dread that ties their knots of worry and despair

Their smiles are extinct as they row with the strangers
Their splayed oars have forgotten time, forcing the boat to slow
So as they spray the reckless waves they convey their voices
As densely harsh as the scream of a child in desperation

They soon relish the golden sweat and solid labour and detest the bitter reluctance
They try to calm their pulsating hearts as the boats split off into groups
And the river is fed teardrops as the fragile spirits plead for change
But the people's anxious cries are worthless because no one can adjust the arrangement

Their once concrete formation has melted and reformed and the groups emerge at ranging distances
Their eyes are heavily hooded as they combat the cascading waves that roar with humid anger
But some bodies are sinking and falling while the strong bodies push them down with their barbed words
Only the bodies with a bulletproof core lie independently on the cooling current

They rescue the bodies that the water has not imprisoned and only the resentful people are unwilling
They start to sway back and forth undecided on whether they want to proceed

And some gain the fruitful knowledge of how to push on to defeat the water
But others in their dark insecurity argue with it until they give up the battle

Their glistening eyes squeal in delight as they approach exquisite land
Their fond farewells echo bubbling ripples in the tide
And their laughter tastes as good as the fresh fruit the island boasts
But after they cross this curve of land their angelic souls are released into the sea

No boat, no life ring, nothing . . .

Lucinda Maitra (13)

BAILEY

They say Marley is the worst dog in the world,
Well they haven't met Bailey yet,
She is the worst dog in the world,
I bet you're wondering why,
Well, she,
Chews my pants,
She digs holes, chases cats,
She annoys Fudge,
I can go on forever
But I love her,
She steals chicken bones out the bin,
Although she's a rescue dog,
That's not an excuse.
She meets dogs that run away
But she only wants to play.
I love her though,
She can be cute,
She can be funny,
I love her with all my heart
And she's mine no matter what.

Alexia Constantine (12)

TIZZY

Although I'm always busy,
My little dog Tizzy,
Stays, sitting in my house,
As quiet as a mouse.

She lays silently on the floor,
And then barks at the dogs next door,
Tizzy is so good,
Just like any other dog should.

She has a best friend called Lucy,
They both are very juicy,
My life is that she's apart,
And she'll stay forever in my heart.

Katy Dixon (12)

SUMMER PEARLS

My summer is yellow
The burnished sand is grated gold.
The sun - a translucent crystal
Smiling in the sky.

My summer is blue
A flawless blanket dotted with clouds
A sea ripples like lustrous velvet
A bed of azure waves.

My summer is green
The lush green leaves of an oak tree
Grass smells as fresh as hope
On my summer's day.

My summer is white
The empty page of a summer poem
The moon - a solid pearl
Watching me in my sleep.

Ellen Blanche Morgan (12)

LITTLE SALLY-MAY

She used to be vibrant and colourful
But now she's just grey

She used to be full of happiness
She was always okay

Everything has changed now
Little Sally-May

When Sally was a little girl
She was a bundle of joy

Now she's full of sadness
Her and that strange little toy

Ever since she got that thing
She has been acting ever so weird

I want my friend back
I want little Sally-May.

Omodolapo Ogunfuye (12)

PONY CARE POEM

There are some problems you can fix,
Like getting rid of your pony's ticks,
Checking his legs for scars and sores,
Sweep the stable and the floors,
A pony owner always should,
Be as trustworthy as an owner could,
Brush his coat and clean his tack,
Keep an eye out for fleas on his back,
Go up to the yard in snow or hail,
To comb his mane and pull his tail,
Check his droppings, for he may have worms,
Clean his water bucket to avoid germs,
Pick out his feet every day,
Make sure he's got plenty of hay,
Feel his body for unusual lumps,
Clean his field so it isn't a dump,
Make sure your pony stays fit
And clean your brushes and grooming kit,
Don't let him eat harmful plants,
Don't overwork him or he will pant,
If he's too cold or starts to sweat,
You may have to call the vet,
Reward good things and not bad,
Make him the best pony you've ever had!

Chloe Blades (12)

THE FINAL FEELING

Bravery, rage, confusion
Darkness, depth, uncertainty
The feeling inside followed by action
The contrast with love, like day is to night.
Love can be magic but magic and illusion.
Translucent, vague, an act.
When anger makes you blind,
The world opens its eyes to see the real you.

Emma Hardy (17)

THE TWILIGHT SAGA

Twilight

T o express love and life
W orld is not what it seems to be
I rrevocably in love with a vampire
L ove is the existence of life
I nexistence Edward and Bella together for ever
G etting to know more about vampires
H atred for Jacob as Bella loses interest
T ogether as a couple the end is not over.

New Moon

N ew beginning, new life
E verlasting love ending
W ishful thinking and wishes gone till the end.

M aking new friends and spreading love to Jacob
O verseeing fears and promises
O pening up her feelings and troubles
N ever say it's too late.

Eclipse

E verlasting love and wars
C atching those who do wrong
L ove gets stronger than ever
I t's the truth to love and wars
P redictions turning every corner
S aving those you love
E nding wars but gaining love.

Breaking Dawn

B reaking news for the Cullens
R elaxing honeymoon becomes a disaster
E ngaged one story, married the next
A gitated the Cullens wait
K illing experiences for Jacob
I mpatience as Bella becomes pregnant
N ewborn vampire is born (Renesmee)
G asping for blood and love.

D esperate for becoming a vampire
A ccepting Edward Cullen forever
W ill it all last forever?
N ow everything's perfect for everyone.

Danielle Carlie Hicks (15)

GRANDMA'S COTTAGE

Grandma's cottage they say it's boring,
But if you dare enter a lot of things can happen.
Your head turns round, you hang upside down
But best of all there's a funfair.
When you eat candyfloss you turn pink,
But when you go in the bathroom you start to sink.
Outside there's the tallest tree house
But when you go inside it's the smallest tree house.
The freakiest thing is her singing!
When you drink hot chocolate it's hot . . .
But I hope not.
There's a roller coaster that's really fun,
But then she goes calm and I have a bun.

Molly Stewart (7)

SUMMER DAY

Summer brings light and sunshine
Bright and clear
Children eating their ice creams
Lots of flavours
Strawberry, chocolate and vanilla
Can you taste the summer day?

Children playing in the garden
Loud and noisy
Mums and dads going crazy
Mums are making strawberry trifle
Sweet, scrummy
In my tummy.

Lots of people having picnics
Happiness and joy
Flowers are blooming
Fragrant and sweet
Do you like the summer day?

Saumya Nath (10)

BENJI THE SOONER DOG

I have got a dog called Benji
He is such a sooner dog
He sniffs and peeks through the hole in the fence
To see if he can see Whiskers, the cat
Benji likes to play peeka-boo with Whiskers, the cat
But Whiskers is an unsociable, typical cat
So Benji has another peep and sniff
To see if he can catch Whiskers, the cat
He likes to be brushed thoroughly through
It sharpens his wits so he can grab that cat
He likes to ride in Dad's big yellow van
Waiting at the door, jumping for joy
To get to the fence to catch Whiskers, the cat
A peep and another sniff in the hole in the fence
But he can't see him 'cause
He is lying on the fence
Snoring!

Jessica Pavitt (13)

UNDERWATER

My heart thunders, my lips are raw
Uncertain, but not unsure.
Encompassing cold around me gains,
Electric shocks pulsing through my veins.
It hugs me close, there's nowhere to hide,
The tang of fear now starts to subside.
Not strangers now, so it plays a game,
Ripples start to sing my name.
I reach out, I call in vain,
No frustration, just hope, so I call again.
Fat, juicy bubbles slide up my face,
But above my forehead they are embraced
By the threads of hair gently stroking my cheeks.
To something deep inside, this world of beauty speaks.
I have the arms of a doll, limp and weak,
The cloud on a blue sky - a plain white streak.
My hammering heart is now a distant drum,
Eyelids shut, surrendering to what is to come . . .

Jessica Wevill (14)

DAYS AND NIGHTS OF LIGHT

As the golden light of day falls down
And clings hopelessly to reluctant clouds.
As the night wind whispers through distant trees,
But no reply from these old
Contemplative souls.
And the fields unto its message spread
As the sun slips down till its light is no more
Down to a different sky
Another sunrise
And other sky
A different time.
To be replaced with darkness
Littered with gleaming diamonds
Or so called stars
And joined in eternal partnership
With the crescent of silver
The inspiring moon.
But itself who inspired by the sun
That same sun which now doth rise
Higher and higher it flies
And sends out the chilled morning breezes
To call out 'good morning arise' to all
And the sun crowns the heavens
But no moon or stars
They have moved on to take the sun's place
In those other skies.
Days fast and days slow
Days filled and empty
Days and nights of light.

Lara Hickson (12)

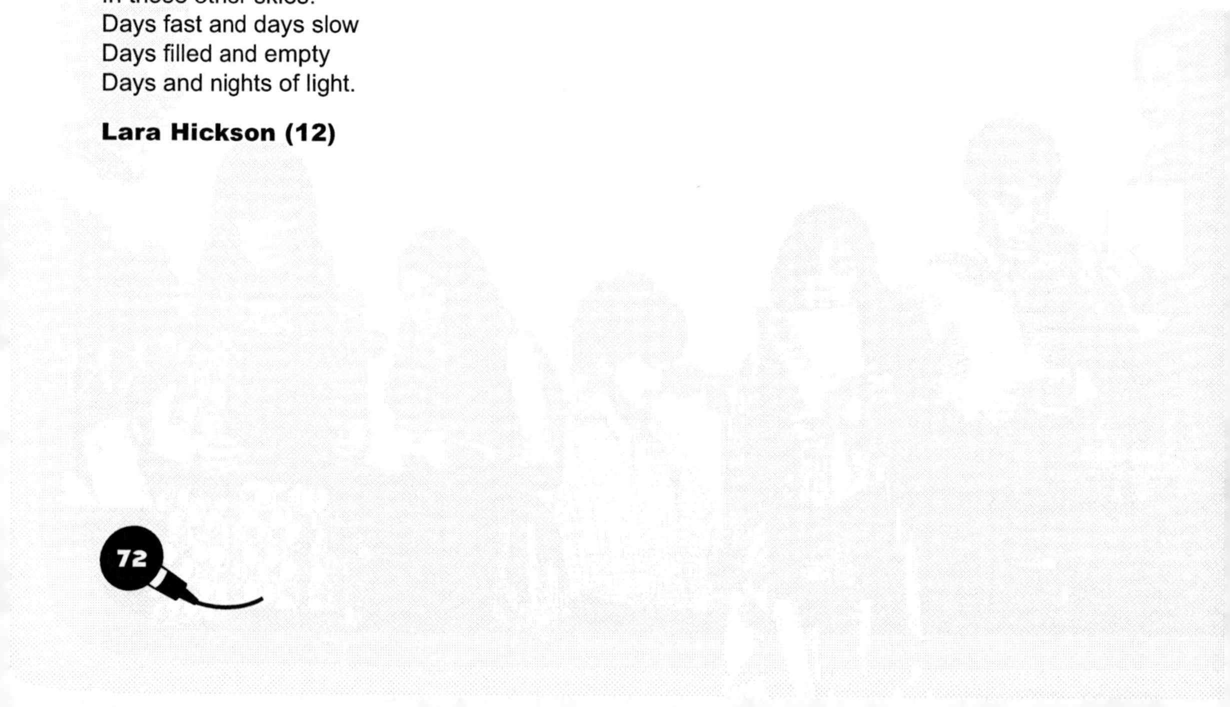

RELEASE FROM PURPOSE

And so God gave the Ten Commandments,
His crowning ultimatum,
The rules to which Man should adhere.
He gave them Heaven for their purpose
And Hell for them to fear,
Lest they do not obey His rules,
Lest they do not revere.

Fools.

All I say is this;
Go out,
Go live,
Go love,
Go give.

But never give your soul,
No never sell your soul.
Not for the hope of Heaven,
Nor for the fear of Hell,
Just keep it yours and keep it whole.

For your life is yours to live
In any way that you should choose,
For no other reason than, it's there to use,
Because . . .
It's not a task.
It's not been lent,
It's not a gift,

It's an event . . .

Life itself is nothing special,
Only a canvas empty, blank.
The one who lives it gives it colour,
They're the one we ought to thank.

And I know you'll find it hard,
Living 'just because'.
Far easier, indeed,
To think life has a purpose.
But I tell you this, my friend,
Understand that living is the goal of life
And yours will be glorious till its end.

Thomas Hother (15)

POPPY

She was only five
This is what did happen
When she was alive

Her dad was a drinker
Her mum was an addict
Her mad parents kept her
Locked in the attic

Her only friend
Was a little toy bear
It was old and worn out
And had many patches of hair

She always spoke to it
When no one was around
She laid there and hugged it
Not a peep of sound

Until her parents
Unlocked the door
Some more and more pain
She'd have to endure

A bruise on her leg
A big scar on her face
Why would she be in such a horrible place?

But she grabbed her bear
And softly cried
She loved her parents
But they wanted her to die

Then one night
Her mum came home high
And poor Poppy was beaten
As hours went by

Then her mum suddenly
Grabbed for a blade
It was sharp and pointy
One that she made

She thrust the blade
Right into her chest
'You deserve to die
You worthless pest'

Then her mum walked out
Leaving Poppy slowly dying
She grabbed the bear
And again started crying

Police showed up
At the small little house
Then quickly barged in
As quiet as a mouse

One officer slowly
Opened a door
To find the little girl
Lying on the floor

It must have been bad
To go through so much harm
But at least she died with
Her best friend in her arms.

Emily Charlotte Henderson (13)

THE GREEN FLASH

The sea was calm,
Not a wave to be seen,
But suddenly on the horizon,
There was a massive flash of green.

It came out of nowhere
And frightened us all to death,
But it also tipped our boat over,
So we all had to take an enormous breath.

The water was freezing,
Cool and refreshing it was not,
So we were all very cheerful,
When land is what we got.

We could just make out,
By the light of the moon,
That we were at Brighton beach
And that help would come soon.

Nowadays,
At exactly midnight,
I journey out to sea
And I still get a fright.

Sachin Bhangra (11)

FLYING BIRD

If love was a flying bird,
I'd always be up there,
Showing everyone I love,
Showing everyone I care.

For if you've got the ability to,
See who you can find,
To love, to care for each other,
For each heart is one of a kind.

Megan Swindell (15)

WHAT'S LOVE GOT TO DO WITH IT?

I don't have much to say
Not really
What can I say?
I love you?
Perhaps not.

It's just another day,
Nothing new,
Just the same old boredom
Same old hurt;
Same old emptiness.

Would it be cruel if I took you
For my own?
It would be, wouldn't it?
But, I was always selfish
Always cruel.
Always abusive.

How do you do it?
Drive me into this insanity?
How can you always smile
Like that
Through all the pain, tears and blood?

I Hate you.
I Despise You.
I absolutely Loathe you.
But you know what I hate the most?
That I Love You.

I hate that I Love You.

Why did it have to be *you?*
You, out of all people?

Because I saved you from yourself.
Besides, I fell in love with you first

What does love have to do with it?

Szilvia Varga (15)

THE STORY OF YOU

The summer sunset fades away,
As the dust starts to settle,
Your heart begins to slow,
As the guns begin to fall.

Who are you anyway?
And what are you fighting for?
Does this mean anything to you?
Do you even care anymore?

If you understand as much as me,
Then you know nothing at all,
So stop lying there on the floor,
Make this your last fall.

There is war behind every door,
So choose wisely my friend,
Don't care for what others think,
Or there'll be another heart to mend.

Who are you anyway?
And what are you fighting for?
Does this mean anything to you?
Do you even care anymore?

I believe you know the answers now,
Well, as much as we all do,
So believe in yourself,
Become the master of you!

Laila Staubmann (12)

LIFE JIGSAW

Hundreds of pieces form a picture made.
Many different shapes put down and laid.
But together some pieces just won't fit,
It must be built bit by bit.

For many others, the purpose the same,
And pieces are added, hardening the game.
It must be done carefully to get it right,
Made of dark colours and also light.

It gets more complicated as it builds,
Makes people feel calm or very chilled.
It may make others angry, frustrated or sad,
While others feel happy and very glad.

Goes on for many weeks and way, way, more
Which is why life is like a jigsaw.
With pieces not fitting and problems so sad,
Dark colours are feelings angered and mad.

Goodness and happiness are feelings so bright,
The picture is life, what a unique sight!
The pieces are experiences as they pass,
Progress is aging, how long to last.

When the jigsaw's complete, this life is then done,
Take it apart, a new one has begun . . .

Abigail Blood (12)

JUST WORDS

Your meaningless words grant me no emotion,
why bother if you see no reaction?
I could stare at your mouth drivel all week
with a blank glare, mind asleep.
If you'd the choice of words or numbers
only a crazed fool would ponder it.
Why dedicate your life to definite answers
while inner beauty flourishes elsewhere?
Mind asleep, the motor roars on endlessly.
How I wish the fuel was less efficient,
yet I seem to be the concern here,
though it seemed his care had expired.
His eyes full of disappointment and restriction,
I wonder how he had come to this.
Had he once been a being of inspiration
that had withered out like a flame?
Though, a sweet realisation,
my procrastination is at its end,
for my love lives with words truly.
My result will be a letter, not a figure.

Alexandra Wallin (16)

CHILD LEFT TO CRY

Echoes and whispers that pass me by,
Beaten down broken child left to cry.
These tears once on my cheeks, have fell to the floor,
Life is so bad I wish to take no more.
Sit in a corner my head buried in my knees,
Stop, stop, I don't want to feel pain any more please.
Her face red with anger and hand raised high,
Keep your mouth shut or I'll give you a reason to cry.
Now don't you dare let my ears hear stop,
Her eyes raging like fire, fear makes my heart drop.
She turns around into the shadow, her laugh roars wild,
As she left behind a beaten down broken child.

Shona-Lee Gallagher (16)

FULL OF FULL

I am a very hopeful person
Sometimes very wishful
Not always beautiful
Occasionally resentful
Usually joyful
I am not always thoughtful
Though I'm normally quite careful
I like being peaceful
And I like being cheerful
And I am also very helpful
At times I can be doubtful
I think the world is wonderful
I know that things are colourful
I mustn't be deceitful
All I know is that I am now full of full
Bountiful
Oh dear!

Kayleigh Poulter (9)

UNTITLED

Are things turning around
Or are you cutting me down?
Places are there,
I just can't reach them,
But I'm bouncing back,
Taking up the slack,
Sorting my life out,
Back and fighting,
Losing my shadow,
With my arrow,
Facing in that direction,
Yes, I'm back. Playing.

Harry Pearson (15)

A CHIP!

My brother brought in a golf club,
And tried to get a score,
But when he tried to do it so,
He banged it on the floor!

When my father saw this all,
He had a great big fit,
He turned angry and quite bright red,
And gave the floor a hit!

He looked around,
But could not see,
One little scratch to be!

He got a great big telescope,
And hoped he'd find a chip,
But we all know he didn't,
And put hands to his hip!

We felt a little sorry then,
About the silly chip,
So we decided kindly,
To get him fish and chips!

'A chip!' he said,
'A chip at last,'
And sent my bro to bed!

Tilda Evans (8)

IT'S WAITING

It waits inside your mind.
It waits for your greatest fears.
It waits until you are weeping
and then it drinks your tears.

It triumphs in your throat,
muffling all your screams.
You may not wish it so,
but it's exactly as it seems.

It waits for your surrender,
because you're too weak to fight.
But dry your eyes it must not win.
Just keep it in your sight.

Stare it in the eyes.
Face it once and for all
because it will be defenceless,
if bravery is your tool.

So take my advice
when you start to see the signs,
because *fear* itself
lurks within all our minds.

Anna Barry (15)

TSUNAMI

I was down at the beach, making most of the sun
Totally oblivious of what was to come
Playing and laughing, everyone was there
We were all so happy, not a worry nor care
When suddenly in the distance, it rose from the sky
It was deep and blue and ever so high
It got closer and closer every breath I took
I called out to my mother, 'Look, look!'
My mother turned round, her face with despair
Filled with worries, filled with care
She stood for a moment, taken over by stun
Until sense came to her, she told me to run
But there I still watched, stuck to the sand
My mother screamed and pulled at my hand
The wave was now only seconds away
Goodbyes to my mother I began to say
The wave was now there just above my head
In a few seconds I'd probably be dead
The wave crashed down on Mother and me
Who knew such force could come from the sea
It swept away trees, it swept away land
I tensed my arm, grasping Mother's hand
But to my surprise, nothing was there
My mother was gone, where was she, where?
I looked in every possible place
But still no sign of my mother's face
My family, my friends, washed away at sea
Everyone gone, all except me
I'm all alone now, nobody's there
No one to help, no one to care.

Hope Taylor (10)

THE GENTLE ONE

You were too lost in your own little dreams
That you didn't hear her everlasting screams
Her lips clamped tight around her lies
She says she's alright? She must be fine
She hides it all behind her eyes
Never letting on how she feels inside
As her friends, they crash, all around her
But she's not like that, she never were
She's brave enough to keep it off show
But I know she needs to let it all go
I wish to hold her close to me
I'll be the one to hear her screams
And all the hurting I will take
Before she's the next one to break
Because I have seen it all before
The strength, the courage, becomes no more
Your whole life, it begins to descend
And for me, it was almost the end . . .

Sophie Drewery (17)

THE EMPTY ROAD

There is always an empty road,
Wherever you seek,
No lorry is dispatching its load.

The whispering wind whips up the dust,
Sending it tumbling and sprawling,
Against the old sign post rust.

Once a highway of magnificence,
Guiding travellers of intelligence,
Now lies cracked and broken.

So if you see an old man in the corner,
Spare a thought for that empty road,
Once a highway of magnificence,
Now a dusty old road,
Engraved with memories it tries to show.

Eleanor Martin (12)

HER NAME WAS SARAH

I knew a girl once her name was Sarah,
Timid and quiet, born in November.
She didn't complain,
She didn't cry,
Not even when she was about to die.
It came as a shock,
Nobody guessed it,
She always was mocked,
Never protected.
If only we knew what was in store,
Before poor Sarah couldn't breathe anymore,
If only she told us what was wrong,
We could have helped her stay strong.
But there wasn't much we could do in the end,
If only I had been Sarah's friend,
I felt so helpless seeing her every day,
I should have reached out and said don't worry it'll be okay.
I knew a girl once her name was Sarah,
Timid and quiet, born in November.
She didn't complain,
She didn't cry,
Not even when she was about to die.
Not even when the cancer ripped her apart,
Not even when it stopped her heart.

Anna Louise Welsh (14)

LIFE UPON A SHELTER'S WAR

Sweeping the tears off my trace,
Feeling the blood over my lace,
Such despair of guilt and hate,
Knowing the funeral of my friend is not late,
Sirens go by; I wait and watch.
In my trenched bed my last touch,
The chilled horrors of a bullet through me,
Keeping my hand on Heaven's keys,
Until it drops so shall I
To fall back up to the sky,
Be a gone person not known to the world.
Not known,
Never known,
Will
I
Really
Ever?

Nabeela Mulbocus (14)

CLOSE MY EYES

I close my eyes
Another universe begins;
Buildings to my design
Skies so blue they confuse the sea

Magic found in impossible places
Magic so frightening yet exhilarating
So powerful yet so gentle
Ideas so conflicting yet make so much sense

I open my eyes
That world that felt so real
Those magical moments felt so sacred
That world that just could not exist

I close my eyes.

Jeanette Wu (16)

ONE MORE SUMMER DAY

Oh, just one more day
One more day of summer please
So I can wake up
To the dancing of sun on my face
To the music of birds outside my window
So I can listen to them tweeting away
Just one more day, so I can still be surprised
By the sand I find
Lurking at the bottom of my shoe

I cry a toast for summer!
To suncream and freshly cut grass
To burnt shoulders and freckled noses
To candyfloss and ice cream
To funfairs and village fetes
Most importantly to the hope summer brings us
That we will have it every year
And, that every year we will take those precious days
For our own!

Claire Healy (14)

HALLOWEEN, HALLOWEEN

Halloween, Halloween, what a big delight,
Halloween, Halloween, what a scary, fearsome fright.

Halloween comes once a year,
I get excited when it comes near.

Everyone has pumpkins near their front door,
And when you get sweets you want loads more!

All the shops have scary decorations,
It more than meets my expectations.

Benjamin Spencer Trill (9)

RUN

With your bloodstained hand in mine tonight
We can carry on alone
Or give up the fight
We can sit and stare as the world ignites
In flames
So beautiful

But can we run forever?
Can we turn back, never?
Can we stay together
Until the angels call?

When the sunlight fades from your hopeless eyes
We can dance together under starless skies
And we can keep on running
Until the day we die.

But can we fight without a gun?
Can we watch the burning sun?
Can the war be won?
No.
But we can run.

Katie Read (13)

THE GIRL FROM THE WOODS

She stood there by the tall oak trees,
Cuts and scrapes across her knees,
The strong wind whipped her face and hair,
Her dress was torn, her feet were bare,
She smiled softly and sang to the breeze,
For she was the girl by the old oak trees,

She had no home according to folk,
Every morning she stood there by the oak,
Waiting for her mother to return,
Seeing her did make my stomach churn,
She waited and waited throughout the year,
No emotions showing, not a single tear.

Isabella Coleman (12)

RUSTAM

You look up at me with big, green eyes,
The sound of your miaow takes me back to a time
When I got to know you for the first time,
Watched you prowl into my life.

You were eight weeks old and so small,
I was scared at first to stroke you,
You seemed so delicate and fragile
And I carefully held out my finger.
Your nose pressed against it
And I knew you liked me.

I watched you grow into a playful furry ball.
Watched you chase after butterflies
But never hurt them.
You used to play with my hands,
Wrestling and fighting but never hurting.
And I'm proud to say you never harmed a thing,
Not a mouse, not a rat, not a bird.

I remember when the stresses of life
Brought me crying into my bedroom . . .
I remember you looking at me
With the same green eyes, understanding.
Your paw on my arm brought me comfort,
Your innocence wiping away tears.

And now, you've grown old.
It is my turn to care for you,
And your turn to watch me grow.
You seem to have outgrown me,
Grown to an adult faster than I have.
From a kitten to a lion, you grew wise.
Now, you are again delicate and fragile,
But I'm no longer scared to stroke you,
Knowing you will always know me,
And I will always know you.

Farhat Raza (15)

THE POWER OF LIFE

Times and events in my life
Moments I'll remember, ones I'll forget,
Some I'll shed tears, others I'll regret,
Many may be fears, because I've been threat.
Most should be my laughter and smile,
Which is so hard to gain,
It usually takes such a while,
Because I'm in great pain.
Times when I have to cry,
Not because I want to, even though I try,
To look forward to my day,
Some people beat you, but that's life . . . anyway,
There's always sometimes
I have a saying, to make life what we need it to be,
Because every day I'm here praying,
If life has a possibility . . .
There's always questions in my mind,
That are so complicated,
And the answers are so hard to find,
When mostly everything in the world is hated.
Life should be peaceful and true,
Life should be clever to help you,
Life shouldn't be greedy, instead it should help the needy,
Life's not what most people want, it's what they need.
This is written in clear font, you need life to succeed.
Remember all of those days,
Remember all those nights, where you got lots of praise,
Or consequences because of fighting for equal rights.
Just let your life flow,
Let it have its own beat,
Hold onto it, don't let go
Because sometimes . . .
Life is a cheat.

Adeela Ahmed (12)

HOME

Everybody has a different home
Not everyone lives the same
Some are rich, some are poor
Some are grand, some are small
Some people have no home at all

A home can be a bench
A shell, an igloo or a den
A home can be a house
A flat, a box, or a pen
A home can be a street
A home can be a tree
A home can be a ship
Or the sand below the sea.

A home can be a kennel
A home can be a barn
A home can be a slum or tent
A home can be a farm
A home can be a hole
A home can be a boat
A home can be a pocket
In an old scarecrow's coat.

A home can be a burrow
A room, a cave, a bed
A home can be a warren
A field, a bush or shed
A home can be the sky
A home can be a shack
A home can be with a family
Or running with a pack

A home, a home, a home
Everyone needs a home.

Emma Dawson (13)

I WISH

I wish . . .
I could speed through my life, money up high,
Popularity there too,
I've a story to tell you . . .

Living in a house, no parents or guidance,
I used to get myself dressed for school,
Homework done, I started
Acting the fool.

I used to see young boys already tooled
Ready to ignite
An ignorant side
Of street rats
Acting like fat cats.

No overstating
Of the lack of a positive mentality
That usually ends up as a fatality.

Young boys, you need to fix up
Education is the key
Why can't you see
It's all about who I be
I'm the future

Representing hard work and dedication
It's me today, you tomorrow
Be somebody that you can follow
Raise your game, don't be ashamed
Of being who you are
I'm in the making
I'm gonna be a star
I wish . . .

Jordan Russell (12)

THE ENVIRONMENT

What do you see out of your eye?
What kind of people do you spy?
What type of ground are you standing on?
What has already been and gone?

Take a look to your right,
Is it a pretty sight?
Maybe there's a flock of angry swans,
Or a musician peacefully playing songs,
It could be a raging, roaring sea,
Or a baby sleeping blissfully,
Is the postie dropping off the morning mail?
Is next door's dog contentedly wagging his tail?
Is there a pretty lady singing, 'Avon calling'
Or is a plane overhead gracefully soaring?
Is there a crack in the pavement allegedly bad luck
Or are you surrounded by mud and muck?
Is it the summer or the autumn time?
Are the first signs of spring beginning to shine?

What about on the left side of you,
Are anybody's dreams becoming true?
There could be an actress who's just got the job
Or an orphan child beginning to sob
Are there crisp autumn leaves crunching under your feet
Or tiny cygnets proclaiming their first tweet?
Is there a heartbroken lover crying out loud
Or a nan choking back tears because she's so proud?
There could be a bride walking down the aisle
Or a face that makes all the pain worthwhile.
Is there fresh snow crunching under your wellies
Or is there a hot bothered man fitting tellies?
Is it the winter or the autumn season?
Is the lake rippling for no apparent reason?

Have you ever wondered about the earth
Or seen the breathtaking sights of new birth?
There is a whole new world beneath our shoes,
That also hurts and gets the summer blues.

Everything has feelings, everything feels,
Do you wonder what you're killing beneath your heels?
What creatures live that we are unable to see?
What creatures are terrified of you and me?

There are so many things so magically designed,
The creator cannot be undermined,
Whatever you believe in, whoever you trust,
Please do this, for you must,
Say thank you for everything the environment includes,
For this is where our story concludes.

Naomi India Preston-Low (13)

EVACUATION

I can remember when I was young
Mum sent me overseas
To stop me from being scared
To find a safe place for me

As my mum placed me in the arms
Of her friend, I saw her cry
I was scared when I left this place
Mum wouldn't make it out alive.

I don't know where my daddy is
He's fighting in the war
I wished that he could see me now
Now that I can crawl.

I have asked Mummy's friend before
'When will Mum come home?'
But she just breaks down in tears
It chills me to the bone.

Although I remember one thing
Back in the time of my youth
When I was in that dreadful place
Mum whispered, 'I will always love you.'

Now that I am older
I know where my parents are
And even though they're not around
They are still here in my heart.

Jadeene Parsons (15)

ANIMALS OF THE WORLD

Animals, animals make me cry
When I see them suffer and die.

Tigers, lions will all be extinct
If we don't use our minds to think.

Their habitat means a lot to me
And to others as you see.

Dogs and cats mean a lot
Even when they lose the plot.

So stop the animals from going away
And help me . . . save the day.

Amy Jenkins (12)

PS I'LL LOVE YOU FOR ALL ETERNITY

It's quite complicated but here it goes,
The things I've learnt - been shown and told,
I was once quite small and had hardly a clue,
The many things that I could do,

I've learnt to walk, laugh and cry,
Developed a sense to be awfully shy,
I found it hard to put into words,
That I had a huge phobia of flies and birds,

I've learnt to smile, talk and scream,
I've grown up so fast - I'm now a teen,
My mother and father taught me many things,
Showed me the happiness our family brings,

Looking back at life I've changed a lot,
I've accomplished things and given them my best shot,
My parents have loved me so caringly and raised me up affectively,
PS I'll love you for all eternity.

Kadife Toci (13)

WITCHES' BREW

Stir in a leg of a frog,
Roast up the body of a dog,
Add in some burnt steak,
Mix in a swan from a lake.

All in the cauldron,
Let's get this done,
Then after that
We'll have some fun.

Chop up an elephant's head,
Stir in some rats that are dead,
Cut off a scorpion's sting,
Drop in a wedding ring.

All in the cauldron,
Let's get this done,
Then after that
We'll have some fun.

Add in a smelly sock,
Heat up a crystal rock,
Mix in some fair hair,
Boil up the face of a mare.

All in the cauldron,
Let's get this done,
Then after that
We'll have some fun.

Mush up a tangled wig,
Toast up a raw fig,
Scrape off some dirty mud,
Pour in some dark red blood.

All in the cauldron,
Let's get this done,
Then after that
We'll have some fun.

Slice up a cat's bottom,
Add some cake which is rotten,
Drop in a human's eye
And make up a lovely pie.

All in the cauldron,
Let's get this done,
Then after that
We'll have some fun!

Madison Preece (10)

AGAINST HOPE

Life has been sucked out of me
For the present time.
I can't concentrate
Can't feel
Can't breathe without you
Around me.
I need you to be there
To help me live
You're my life support
My everything
And I can't help but feel
That you could maybe
Feel the same.
Wishful thinking
I know, can lead
To false hopes
And heartache
But
I'm hoping
This time it's real
Hoping
Against hope
That you'll let me in
To your heart too.

Emma Rickard (17)

I AM A CARROT

I am a carrot
I live in a drawer
I'm getting old
I've got some mould
When I sit in the dark
All I ever hear is the dog
Bark, bark and bark
And I wonder why I haven't been eaten yet
I am a carrot
I live in a drawer
I'm getting old
I've got some mould
When they open the fridge
They look around
They pick me up so I smile
But then they put me down so I start to frown
I am a carrot
I live in a drawer
I'm getting old
I've got some mould
Every time they open the fridge they look fatter than before
Don't you understand without me you will be fat

Forever.

Grace Prudhoe (11)

THE VIKINGS

The Vikings were dangerous, the Vikings were scary,
The Vikings were strong and the Vikings were hairy.

The Vikings were warriors, they searched for no peace,
The Vikings were vicious, just like hissing geese.

The Vikings were brave and the Vikings were bold,
The Vikings were traders that swapped things for gold.

The Vikings were evil, full of bloodthirsty gore,
If you asked me to name one, then I would name Thor.

Vikings were famous for their brilliant boats,
So no need to panic, I assure you they float.

The Vikings were spies, a bit like James Bond,
They had one thing in common, they were all very blonde.

The Vikings will live on in me, although we've never met,
I swear I shall remember them and never will forget.

Joseph Woods (11)

TONIGHT, BE CLOSE TO ME

Musical sweethearts,
watch them march by,
night has gone,
she wished them goodbye,
and smiles were all round,
money earned, let's have a toast!
Red brick . . . red brick . . . hushed,
usuality is stripped away,
like the English cloud hanging above.
Stumbling on turned up maroon
they exclaim, 'Oh it's sore down here,
albeit you can see the stars.'

Rachel Dickson (16)

MY IDEAL WORLD

My ideal world
Would not be curled
It would be hard, flat and square
And all of life would be fair.

Mankind may stay
Mankind may go
Which one I would choose
I just don't know.

Follow the path to reach your goal
Step off this road and lose your soul
Achieve this goal and go to Heaven
Where you'll stay 24/7
Be good and truthful throughout your time
And in your next life there will be no crime.

Only animals cute and fluffy
None of them can be scruffy;
Bunnies, monkeys and some dogs
Hippos, elephants, but not hogs.

If you lie and cheat your way through life
Then after death you'll get the knife
If you've been naughty, locked in a cell
Then you shall be condemned to Hell
Forever and ever you shall stay
Reliving that unforgiving day.

One religion is all there can be
This is what people cannot see
A war for resources soon will come
This is certain; second to none.

Darren James Lee (17)

ASLEEP

I sit, childlike,
My heart head cushioned by your heartbeats
Breathing in the smooth slow rhythm of your body
Aware in the sleepless house
Of a far deeper intimacy
Than the comical act we shared
A short time ago.
Against the luminous linen sheet
I watch your hand
Fern-fist furled
Grasping your dream as time flows by.

Soon, I will rise
Button on yesterday's shirt,
Buckle my belt,
Tie the laces of my silent shoes,
Shadowy witnesses to our ridiculous ritual.
I will smoke a cigarette in your kitchen
Shivering in the pre-dawn chill
And leave on the table
A semi-apologetic note
Captured under the vase with the roses I gave you
A thousand breaths ago.

But as I slip away
With dawn and my thoughts
Accompanying the sleek hum of my car
I shall not think of you
Finding me gone,
Remembering our brief promises and ludicrous laughter.
You finding my note -
Half regretful, half relieved.

I shall be thinking
Of the smell of your hair when you're asleep,
The secret hollow behind your ear
Where your dreams are kept,
The passages,
Hidden staircases,
And fairy tale towers
Where I was briefly your guest
In the intimate dark
Before dawn.

Naomi Gardom (16)

FATHER TIME

Father Time
I can't tie your hands,
You wander centuries alone,
Through raging storms and blistering sands.

With the power of the hourglass,
Firm within your grasp,
Coated in ancient wisdom,
A paragon of the past.

Never changing,
Forever frozen,
A figment of what once was.
Photographs engraved in memory,
Capable of moving on, longing, but never does.

Darkness draws on,
Your hands wind down,
Fate encloses,
Yet you wear no frown.

Time, you take no vengeance,
No judgement passes your lips,
No bitter grudge beneath your breath,
Just endless dwindling ticks.

Time, you wait for no man,
Myself am no exception,
You watch as people waste your gift,
Searching for 'perfection'.

When ice meets fire, sun meets moon,
All we know is gone,
Lost in oblivion, wandering entity,
Yet time still lingers on . . .

Siân Delin (14)

TO MY LOVE

I am writing a poem just for you,
So show me a smile to help me through,
I don't know how much I mean to you,
But I just have a few things to say to you!

Every time I see your face,
You take me to another place,
Somewhere where I feel safe and strong,
Somewhere with you is where I belong!

I would just like to say that,
To see you every single day,
Would make me happy for eternity,
Because guess what? I love you!

I love you with all my heart,
I hope you feel the same way too,
I will see you through,
Everything and anything that happens to you,
Now, forever and every single day,
Thinking, alone in my bed I lay!

You complete me in every single way,
And now I've said that what more is there left to say?
Apart from I love you with all my heart,
And I hope we never break apart!

Sarah March (15)

THE EARTH AND THE MOON

The sighing Earth longs for the moon
That floats in space bound by its orbit,
And dreams; defying gravity
And sleeps; among the stars.

In all those wakeful hours, tired
Earth keeps turning with the tide
And pouring over dark abyss, her
Eyes are open wide.

What silence in those craters formed?
What peace lies in the dust,
That settled many years ago
When moved by glory's thrust?

What glory? Glory did forsake her
Barren craters bare.
They too were born of force and fire
Yet now cry with despair.

What of all the fresh green blades of grass,
Martyrs supreme,
Of causes bearing change,
That flush of red of faded dreams.

And all the pools of shining jewels that
On reflection gave delight
Cannot wash her bloody fools
Or curb the mighty smiter's smite.

She hangs upon a stardust thread,
And still breathes light amidst the dark,
Broken; crust is wafer thin and
Crippled, yet not dead.

Amen, be still, peace be with thou,
The prayers of Jupiter and of Mars
And echoed through the galaxy -
You shall sleep among the stars.

Katherine Giddins (17)

PERFECTION BEHIND THE EYES

When I close my eyes,
Happiness floods the dark space,
Lighting it up with softness,
Crowding it with peace in a beautiful place.

I see the world and the people there,
I'm flying over pure civilisation,
I'm curing diseases and starving starvation itself,
And it's unaware.

The wars are loud and disturbing below,
I'm stopping the blood and the pain,
I'm seeing tears of joy,
Here are the survivors without a foe.

For those who think their lives are in vain,
I'm marring it with hope and sadness is put to shame.

The victims of abuse are calling out in their sleep,
I'm mocking the disturbed mind,
I'm letting them forget,
Hoping that their new option of happiness is for keeps.

Mother Nature has again shown her style,
Creating earthquakes and flooding,
I'm going back in time,
Stopping her thoughtless antics for a while.

For those who think they are so alone,
From me their lost friends and family are shown.

The murdered people are screaming in their graves,
Tormented by their lost innocence,
I'm digging them up from Hell,
Their flesh is reborn and how beautiful are their waves.

The homeless people who have nowhere to go,
Their brains full of misery and regret,
I'm giving them money and food,
Taking them away from their all time low.

For those who have always had a hole in their heart,
I'm letting them kill Cupid by ripping his bad decisions apart.

The children who have been kidnapped and stabbed without a sound,
Their lives taken before they had begun,
I'm killing the killer first,
The disgusting plot of the murderer is never found.

The animals are talking in different voices,
But they know their lives are being taken for us,
I'm opening the factory doors,
Who are humans for making all these choices?

For every living creature who has ever been hurt,
I'm giving them life eternal and throwing all bad things into the dirt.

But just when I think I have cured everything and everyone,
Numbed the grieving,
Shown all of them the light and the sun,
I open my eyes.

Octavia Brayley (14)

ADIEU, AUF WIEDERSEHEN, GOODBYE

Sink your feet into the sand,
Look ahead and take my hand,
Softly wipe those trailing tears,
While the waves wash away your recurring fears.
When the winter comes and goes,
Not a soul, no one knows
The way you mourn, the way you cry,
I will not stay to say goodbye.
As spring comes the flowers bloom,
Walk away my dear, from the impending doom.
Graves in sequence, faces lost,
I will miss you the most.
And then the summer is in view,
Birth to life, a world anew.
Cherish the moments yet to come,
Remember to love me, some.
Collective breaths are heard from above,
A shaky cry, sounds too tough.
And then you leave the chrysanthemums,
I assure you, I'm in peace and calm.

Farhana Begum (17)

THE LAMPLIGHT DANCER

Have you ever wondered what the lamplight dancer could be?
Well just wait and see . . .

She is a spark, sent from the elves,
When the world was in dark despair.

As soon as she came into our world,
Happiness spread around mankind.

Many heard of her,
So as a gift they made lamp posts, named lamplights.

One saw her dance on the lamplight,
Giving her the name 'The Lamplight Dancer'.

Two lucky people see her each generation,
As I did this night, seeing her grace and great light!

Dylan Savage (9)

WHAT WOULD I BE?

If I wasn't me, what would I be?

I'd be a star,
That twinkled through the night,
Gazed at from below,
And burning beautiful and bright.

I'd be the sun,
Lighting up the sky,
Shining from above,
And ruling up on high.

I'd be the sea,
Calm and blue,
Embracing the shore,
And clear enough to see through.

In fact I would be anything, just to be near you.

Catherine Butterfield (14)

UNTITLED

Shall I compare you to the shining sun?
I think you are a bright ray of sunshine
And yet soon you will be gone
This will be when I am in Year 9
Sometimes, I pray you will not go away
And during the night, I don't get any rest
And yes I know I am afraid to say
That you going to university is for the best.
Yet when I think about you all the time
Although, you like to play the game 'Mercy'
I do not think about that in my mind
Instead, I think of you going to university
And much like the bright sun low in the sky,
You will soon say goodbye.

Joyce Osejindu (12)

THE RED LIPPED WOMAN

The red lipped woman,
What will she do next?
To get what she wants,
Oh, that evil red lipped woman.

She rides in the fear of the night,
Waiting to lure in her next fool.
Her looks impressing them all,
Her mind full of tricks.

With her leather jacket she's as cool as cucumber,
Her name known far and wide.
By victims who have witnessed,
Oh, that evil red lipped woman.

Everything is not what it seems with her,
Just a pretty face for show.
As her mighty weapon,
Proving to be most powerful.

Her plans so deceiving,
Yet so well thought out.
An outlaw, even a highwayman,
You name the title, she owns it,
Oh, that evil red lipped woman.

Knock, knock, knock, at the door,
A lonely girl with not a penny to her name.
A tear will fall, you'll be tempted,
Soon she'll be in your territory.

First, they'll be signs, then the gestures,
Then comes the looks and then a kiss upon your cheek.
You'll be hooked like a fish,
Oh, that evil red lipped woman.

She'll give you everything you want,
All your dreams fulfilled,
Then stab you in the back and you'll have . . . nothing.

Next comes the dispute,
And then the warning,
And then the gun to your neck,
Then she'll leave, leaving you with a red kiss upon your cheek,
Oh, that evil red lipped woman.

So if you hear a knock,
Don't go, you're falling into a trap.
Just remember . . .
The red lipped woman never stops until she gets what she wants,
Oh, that evil, evil red lipped woman.

Tiah Rebecca Shepherd (10)

MY HORRIBLE LIFE

This is my life as you can see
Luck for them but none for me.
All around me I see hugs and kisses
But for me it's hisses.
No one cares
I wish they were eaten by bears.

This is my life as you can see
Other children shouting for glee.
I just sit in a dark room
Waiting for doom,
Not one hug
Or tucked in nice and snug.

This is my life as you can see
I'm stuck here for all eternity.
I wish someone could step in my shoes
All my friends would lose.
I'm not here anymore
So shut the door.

Sapphire Lennan (10)

HAPPY FATHER'S DAY

You are my father,
And I love you in every way
Every father deserves to hear this
So happy Father's Day!
You take me out on trips,
You tell me jokes along the way
When you arrive back from work,
I shout, 'Hip hip hooray!'
We are as close as can be,
You love me like no other
You always give me the warmest hugs,
I couldn't wish for anything better
When I say that I love you,
I say it from the bottom of my heart
I will never let anything happen to you,
I will hate for us to ever be apart.

Nidaa Mahmood (10)

THE WRITER'S MEDITATION

Staring blankly at a blank page
In a room where the grimy windows
Let in little light.
Your pen poised, trembling, in mid-air,
As if ready at any moment to touch something
That isn't quite there.

Deep crinkles seem to be etched
Into the sky around your mouth -
A thousand tiny lines of concentration
Running from head to chin,
Forming crevices skin deep.

Miniscule beads of sweat cling
To face and hair, giving the appearance
Of a recent shower, but the gentle sway
Of your thoughts carries on -
Unaffected by heat and tiredness.

And when you eventually fall,
Exhausted, into your bed,
Cushioned by the gentle warmth
Of your covers, you suddenly realise
That you have yet to write that magnificent first word.

Ellie Fisher (11)

WHY OH WHY DO WE HAVE A HEART?

To help us live
To help us run
To help us move or
To love and care
To help us find the one true love we seek
To help us fulfil our most deepest desires
To make the right choice so our heart doesn't ache
To make sure our heart doesn't break
To keep hope even in the darkest of places or
To leave room for yourself, if you get lost along the way
Your heart is always there for you until the day you die.

Divya Sharma (12)

COLD DARK CORNER

There's a cold dark corner,
In the back of my room.
It speaks to me,
And says I'm coming for you.

As I lay on my bed,
In the foetal position.
My eyes are closed,
Hoping and wishing.

Maybe that one day,
My dreams will come true.
That I don't have to be here,
So down and blue.

The corner keeps talking,
About how I'm going to die.
And all I can do,
Is lie there and cry.

As the corner gets closer,
It takes me in.
My soul starts to burn,
And so does my skin.

My bones shall lie there,
Turning to dust.
My bed surrounding,
Nothing but rust.

Danielle Martin (14)

MY BEST FRIEND

He was playful,
He wasn't harmful.
We never had an argument,
Even at a bad moment
He was my best friend.

He never hurt my feelings,
But then I had to go away,
So I slowly drove off on a highway
Away, away, away.
I never saw him again, my best friend . . .

I felt solemn and sad,
Everything was bad.
One day I found a letter,
That did not make me feel better,

We had to go to war.
War's the door to death and pain,
And losing all your friends,
You feel that you want to abstain,
But will come back from war bends,

Without your friend.

I hear the echoes of his voice,
Had so much respect for him,
I feel I am sad, we had no choice,
I think I am still with him.

For the rest of my life it seems
But I am not, it's just dreams.

He was my best friend.

Jakub Müller (11)

THE LION AND THE UNICORN

The lion and the unicorn were fighting for the crown,
And whilst doing this, they were making quite an awful sound.
All the animals in the village were asked to choose sides,
The ones who didn't were considered to have silly minds.
'All those in favour of the lion?' shouted the judge at high court.
The cat family, the hippo, the elephant, the bear
And the parrot all chose this sort.
'All in favour of the unicorn?' shouted the judge at high court.
The horses, the dove, the peacocks, the insects
And the humans chose this sort.
The lion's army hid in the forest, waiting to ambush and not to retrieve,
Whilst the unicorn's army discussed how to deceive.
The unicorn's army walked and walked,
While the parrot from the lion's army heard them talk.
'The enemy is coming!' shouted the parrot with glee,
'Then let's get ready for war!' said thee.
The war then started, with the lion's beasts around,
Then the humans appeared, and chased away the beasts without a sound.
The lion's army started to bite and claw,
Although the unicorn's insects were not a bore.
The insects buzzed and buzzed all around the lion,
They buzzed and buzzed and sounded like a siren.
The war between the crown had gone too far, even if not fun,
And nobody even remembered why the war had begun.
Until, alas the turtle, which was on neither side,
Began to start his mighty slow stride.
While the two armies were fighting each other,
No one even noticed the turtle, not one or another.
The slow, slow turtle walked bravely toward the crown,
And shook on the beam until the crown on top fell upside down.
The crown had fallen upon his head,
And so the turtle took in a long breath and said,
'Animals, humans, listen to me!
You are now looking upon the new king's identity!'
The animals turned and looked, all quite happy now,
That the war had stopped, so the new king took a bow.
The lion and the unicorn, so filled with shock,
That they both fell down limp, like a hazy old rock.
'Although they are not dead,' the new king said,
'We must help them recover to their original state.'
'Must we?' cried the crowd. 'Must we let them get back
To their original state?'
And this I tell you, was a quite a debate.

So the new king decided on one rule,
That the village was to keep quiet about the animals who were fooled.
So the lion and the unicorn, as happy as could be,
Set off for a new life, with no other memory.

Jamisyn Perry (12)

REST IN PEACE

(In loving memory of the martyrs of the church burning and of the bloodshed of innocent Christians, rest in peace)

My friend, my relative,
You've worked so hard,
With the sweat of someone being barred,

Where are you now?

My friend, my relative,
It pains me to see,
What they have done to you and me,

Where are you now?

My friend, my relative,
The gates of Heaven departs,
While there are tears prowling in our hearts,

Where are you now?

My friend, my relative,
Your races, they have betrayed you,
When they are really repaying you,

Where are you now?

My friend, my relative,
Death smiled at you,
And God brought you through,

Where are you now?

My friend, my relative,
We all mourn,
But you have just been born,
In a new place beyond here,
With your departed so very near,

Where are you now?

My friend, my relative,
Why won't they stop?
Destroying our religion hoping to succeed,
While bringing us closer,
Then a newborn seed,

Where are you now?

I can tell you where you will be,
Somewhere as beautiful as the sea,
With all your friends,
That have had their ends,
They've tried their best,
And taken their rest,

You will be there now.

So close your eyes,
And say goodbye,
As we look and cry,
You are under God's merciful eye,
As the people who you will be meeting,
Will have been worth the beating,

You are there now . . .

Daniel Mosaid (16)

A CURSED SUN

His face is dark like the night,
His eyes are lifeless, not bright,
Standing in what seems a queue,
He knows he's next, he's due.

The air smells of smoke and burning flesh,
He closes his eyes and begs to be blessed,
Then they dance around the body,
While shouting, 'Which of you Negros is next?'
Stumbling he closes his eyes,
There was no time to even cry,
As his life was lynched out of him . . .

And so, there stood the cross,
It was the white demon's sun,
And so,
The Ku Klux Klan,
Has begun . . .

Maria Ferreira (16)

A TRAIN

I go really fast underground,
With lots of sights to see
I make a strange sound,
Which makes everyone know it's me.

Working every day seems kind of tough,
The same routine goes along,
People get on and off,
Like a little song.

I can help save the Earth
With not much pollution,
Just come with me
And we'll think of a solution.

Sima Jaf (13)

THE FOREST

Running
Don't stop running
I feel the forest floor beneath my pads
The power of the forest flowing through me
My limbs get stronger with each stride
This is the run of a wolf

Soaring
Don't stop soaring
I feel the cold, fast wind beneath my wings
The power of the night flowing through me
I hear the flap of my great wings
This is the flight of an eagle

Tracking
Don't stop tracking
I feel the strength of my bow and arrow
The power of the hunt flowing through me
The arrow wisps through the wind hearing the prey fall
This is the hunt of a hunter.

Eleanor Sollitt (13)

SOLITARY CONFINEMENT

Sat in a corner, covered in pitch-black
For your eyes are useless in this darkness
You're helpless, blind, like the cat in the sack
Peer all you want, but the winner, thankless
The longer you're there, you think that it lifts
It's your imagination, nothing more
Unforgiving darkness is relentless
In this blindness, you can't know which way's shore
Suddenly, and without warning, it lifts
It has not gone, so why is it waning?
You feel a rise within your excitement
You've gone mad, in solitary confinement.

Laura Beswick (16)

SECRETS

Secrets hidden
all around.
Secrets hidden
never found.
Secrets hidden
in your face.
Secrets hidden
ev'ry place.
Secrets hidden
all around.
Secrets hidden
never found.

Secrets hidden
in the stars.
Secrets hidden
behind bars.
Secrets hidden
tightly locked.
Secrets hidden
make me shocked.
Secrets hidden
in the stars.
Secrets hidden
behind bars.

Secrets hidden
in your mind.
Secrets hidden
end of time.
Secrets hidden
in the sky.
Secrets hidden
'til you die.
Secrets hidden
in your mind.
Secrets hidden
end of time.

Secrets hidden
under floors.
Secrets hidden
behind doors.
Secrets hidden
down below.

Secrets hidden
never show.
Secrets hidden
under floors.
Secrets hidden
behind doors.

Secrets hidden
break so soon.
Secrets hidden
kill and wound.
Secrets hidden
all your fears.
Secrets hidden
many years.
Secrets hidden
break so soon.
Secrets hidden
kill and wound.

Secrets hidden
must protect.
Secrets hidden
make you vexed.

Secrets hidden -
do I know?
Secrets hidden -
do I show?
Secrets hidden
must protect.
Secrets hidden
make you vexed.

A bee's nest hidden in the tree.
A bug hidden under leaves.
A star, gone behind a cloud.
A whisper in the noise so loud.
A robin in the blackbird's nest.
A ship, sunk under water's crest.
A murmur, right behind your back,
Getting ready to attack.

Lock it up, throw out the key -
No one knows that about me!

Secrets hidden -
distant shores.
Secrets hidden -
mine and yours.
Secrets hidden -
in your heart.
Secrets hidden -
in the dark.
Secrets hidden -
all endures.
Secrets hidden -
I know yours!

Anna Grant (14)

LIVING

Is it real?
Leaves resting in piles on the ground,
The weather cooling,
Children wrapped up warm,
Running amok,
Making a mess,
Wherever they go,
The snowflakes fall,
Clumping together,
Resting,
Forming a blanket on the icy floor,
The snowmen melting,
Still smiling with their pebble eyes,
And carrot nose,
Wrapped with a scarf,
Children clustering around fires,
Toasting their toes,
Drinking cups of chocolate,
Staying up for when St Nicholas comes,
With a jingle of bells,
And a hearty ho, ho, ho!
Is it there?
The trees blossoming,
Little buds of pink and white,
Opening in the sunlight,
The birds chirping,
Bringing worms back to the nest,
Picnics in fields and parks,
Trips to the seaside,
Ice cream dripping,
As the children lick,
Sunburn glowing red,
On happy faces,
As they dip in cool pools,
Places visited,
Friendships created,
First days and last days,
Little smiles, big grins,
Furrowed brows, open mouths,
Memories made.

Lauren Jones (14)

THAT SUNDAY FEELING

That Sunday feeling is clammy,
It reeks of enforced indolence.
It wheezes miserably as it is throttled by an atmosphere
of rancid peace.

That Sunday feeling is a heavenly hell
which suffocates your senses.
Leaving you with the bitter taste
of stale pleasure.

That Sunday feeling is a dull melody
that sends you to a restless slumber.
While you sleep it infects your organs with a fungus
of fatigued regret.

Stagnant Sunday penetrates your cold dry pores
and numbs you with its stuffy warmth.
It infects like damp your sluggish soul and its mouldering fruits
poison your dulled spirit.

Soon it will be Sunday every day.

Buddleia Maslen (16)

HIDDEN BEAUTY

Stepping one foot in front of the other;
gravel lay on the floor as a cover.
The dusk sky cries;
wet acid tears.
Yet it frees my mind;
the waves of calm, so clear.
The smell of damp garden grass;
pulling the hairs in my nose.
The sighs of the Earth;
seeping up through my toes.
Everything so shady;
collided with mist.
Love in its prime;
with uses of an endless list.

Yasmin Argent (14)

TEARS

Every night beyond the pellucid star-studded sky,
A cry of a thousand tears are shed.
Though summer appears in the month of June,
Rarely compensates what sorrow has said.
For no one can hear the frequency of the sound,
Yet distinguish the weight - a pound?

A million miles away in distance,
The same outcry is heard in the hearts of many.
One of anguish and shame for instance,
Another is resentful of the undertakings of life,
Of disasters and distress of our everyday lives,
What tears our world cries.

Through your eyes I see every element of emotion,
I see the glimmering of joy at scarce times,
Occasionally a smile or similar sort of notion,
Joyful like the words of a children's nursery rhyme.

Listen to the cries of the night.

Mabel Osejindu (17)

COCO GONE UP HIGH, WITH LOVE

Coco, oh Coco, I hope you're okay,
Why did you have to go when I was not ready?
I really want God to let you come back,
Just for one more day,
Then I can stroke your fur and listen to your barks,
I want to hold your paw
And soon I'll let you back through your Heaven door.
Tilly, your sister is all alone,
Probably wishing you could come back home,
No other dog in the house to talk to her in dog language,
Can you hear me right now 'cause I'm singing for you,
Please don't let me cry now you're in the sky,
Let the angels look after you, my little uncle dog Coco.
I love you so but now I'm going to go,
Miss you doggy, Coco.

Natalie Perkins (9)

CONCUSSION

Crack of sunlight
Moths flickering in the silence
Crawling on my skin
Eating away
Disjointed white noise
Flightless birds
Flying away

Pupils dilate
The world distorted
Contortions of a lazy puppeteer
Words fall from tongue
Languishing
Reproachful in the dark

Drowning in drowsiness
Fists clenched too tight
Outlines of pills etched on palms
The blood flow still and solid
Vision aching
Mind breaking
Footsteps tracing

Memories piled high
Nameless faces
Bleached on the shores of nausea
Twists and turns
Chaotic ballet
Precise and wild
Heartbeat echoing
Hollow head
Cloudy head
Scattered showers
And rainy skies

You wonder why
The noise doesn't stop
The tempo doesn't drop
Body arches and buckles
An anchor
A locked cage
The flames flicker

Threatened
Curling on the wax
Undecided
Descending to delirium

Questions jump and stutter
Derailed trains
Car crash
Screeching of a thousand tyres
Screaming of a million shipwrecks
Symphony of rain
Hitting closed windows

A crack
It seeps in
Ghostly invader
Pale surrender
Nothing to remember.

Claire Smith (14)

THEY'RE HERE

Boom! Crash! Bang!
The siren wails out.
Suddenly light arrives,
Showing dead corpses,
It has begun.
Devastation, like an
Armada of explosive bombs.
Rubble all around the fiery
Smoky, blazing night sky.
Hornets in the air, buzzing like
Power-hungry maniacs.
Policemen bawling,
The worse nightmare.
Stars bejewelled,
Emblazoned in
The night sky.
Wishing for all hope,
To end this
Apocalypse.
Smelling the aroma
Of silence and fear,
Making changes in
People's lives.
Waiting for their demise.
Kaboom!
Another couple of
Fools down.
Anger rising in my head.
Our town
Was destroyed.

Estanislao Miles (10)

THE MENTAL EYES, IN DISGUISE!

It's decreasing, my emotional stability
Creating a world of invisibility.

Masking my breaths from reality,
Creating a world of complete misery.

I'm caged in, no escaping,
The blood from my scars is the only hope,
From a world in a state,
I just can't cope.
The torture, the pain,
I feel attached to a chain.
Will I ever feel free again?

You can see my darkened eyes,
With a sparkle of hope in disguise,
I'm still in here, I'm fighting,
I am still alive.

I'm hearing it again,
The hope and love deep inside,
I'm ready to face the world now,
Take the rocky ride.
Let me show you,
I may be misunderstood,
Locked inside a hospital,
But I'm intelligent and capable.

Like today, I am free from the chain,
I am me again,
Two years down the line,
I'm holding my ground,
I'm staying around,
A born survivor, a complete warrior.

Megan Coleman (17)

THE SWAN

Tomorrow's come and I draw near
The river's edge to see a swan,
Too elegant for ponds like these
That crumble 'til there is no more.
He cranes his neck and shrieks out high
His angelic wings beat, he says goodbye.

Too many times I've seen him fly
Away from me only to come back,
Tired and hungry, apologise,
The same thing happens every time.
Though I give him everything he wants
Too beautiful to care too much.
He scopes his wings out full to see
A snow white angel as beautiful as he . . .

Too long did I believe he cared
But no swan so handsome
Would dare to show love
To a duck to compare to his beautiful coat
He loved it too much, he didn't see pain
That it caused the duck who was left behind
In that river. Where he left her.
When he said goodbye.

Megan Koss (16)

TWO LOVERS

Two lovers on a bench,
Sitting side by side,
Stroking each other's trembling hands,
As their hearts collide.

If all this London city love was to ever last,
They'd sit there in the smog and dirt forgetting about the past.

Lee Hayes (17)

ONE IN THE SAME

If I gave him my eyes would he see the way I do?
If I gave him my voice would he speak like I do?
If I gave him my ears would he listen the way I do?
If I gave him my legs would he stand up like I do?
If I gave him my brain would he think the way I do?
If I gave him my heart would he feel or love like I do?

We are one in the same.
Different genders it may be
But we both have eyes
And we both see.

And don't we all have ears
To listen to those who speak
Or do we just pretend
And look for help which we do not seek?

What about the ones who talk?
Don't we all have choices
Or can't we make our choices carefully,
The ones with all the voices?

Are we all just sheep in a herd?
Don't we all have legs to stand up?
You need to be listened to
We aren't just dregs in a blue and green cup.

We are most definitely not clones
We have our own mind, our own brain.
People have to think for themselves.
Stop being wasteful, don't use them in vain.

I am not a robot,
I have feelings and a heart.
So why don't you treat me like an equal.
So please take care of me, make a start.

If I gave him my eyes would he see the way I do?
If I gave him my voice would he speak like I do?
If I gave him my ears would he listen the way I do?
If I gave him my legs would he stand up like I do?
If I gave him my brain would he think the way I do?
If I gave him my heart would he feel or love like I do?
If I gave you these things would you take and take care of them?

Jennifer Howell (17)

LOVE NEVER DIES

Love is true
Love is you
Day by day
I see you.
Day and night
I wait for you.
Someone like you
Is someone like me.
I wish this day never ends.
This is my heart
This is my soul
You are the one
You are the one and only
That my heart thinks of.
Love is justice and peace
And I am justice
And you are peace.
For evermore
We shall be.

Paul Paul (9)

SUMMER

The sky is blue, bright and sunny.
Days get longer and longer.
Leaves bright green.
Flowers are colourful.
Birds twittering and flying here and there.
Children playing, screaming,
Eating ice cream outside.
People are gardening.
The moon is bright and visible at night.
I'm Summer.

Hithara Subasinghe (7)

A NEW BEGINNING

You find it where the sky
touches the earth,
where night meets day.

It is found through hate
and despair,
lost through love
and happiness.

Seen only by those
who seek it,
forgotten by those
who do not dream.

It is the mountains that
carry the magnificent sky,
it is the earth that
supports all given options.

Touchable only when
the moon is partnered
with the sun, and
the grass is floating
atop the sea.

It is the spirit
that fills our souls,
it is the blood
that runs in our veins.

Life.

Jade Siddall (16)

MUSIC

Music is a part of everyone's lives
Bees even have music in their hives
The humming, the whistling, the making of a tune
You know your favourite song will be on the radio soon
The song that everyone sings along to,
Doesn't matter if it's bad or good
You would do anything to be on that stage if you could
The lead guitarist, the drums, the bass,
The smile that you put on everyone's face
Those heart-warming lyrics that feel a part of you
The legendary guitar riff you want to play too
Comparing your favourite bands with your friends
Hoping that the song you're listening to never ends
Feeling like you are in your own special land
While you rock out with the members of the band
As you dance to the beat and wave your hands in the air
You suddenly realise it's a moment you want to share
So you grab your friends and show them what you're passionate about
As you chant with the audience, who cares if you have to shout?
You jump up and down on the spot and start to rock without a care
You're watching a gig outside,
You can feel the cold breeze through your hair
The music vibrations enter your ears and travel round your soul
I love music, my favourite is rock and roll.

Emily Hendy (15)

SPECIAL BOND

A mother and daughter's bond is something you can't replace.
Being there for each other, making sure you're both safe.

Knowing you have got a place to go if you need advice
Makes you feel really nice with a warm glow inside
To know you're both by each other's side.

Lauren Cash (13)

EVERYTHING I WANT

He is everything I want,
A dream, a reality,
A Prince Charming on a horse.

He's touched my heart,
He's touched my soul,
He's everything I want and much, much more.

His dreamy blue eyes,
Take me to another world,
His cute smile,
Just makes me blush.

I wish I could have him forever,
Because this is not just a crush.

He's something I want,
He's something I need,
As without him I am just incomplete.

Because he's everything I want,
A dream, a reality,
A Prince Charming on a horse.

Nabeeda Bakali (15)

MY BROTHER

I'm fixed and formed because of my brother.
He's moulded my life more than another.
People may laugh and think it's a joke,
But he's always there to help me through the smoke.
If ever I'm melancholy or drifting down,
He summons a smile where there once was a frown,
If he had to trek through a treacherous storm,
He'd make sure he's there by the break of dawn.
Our personalities match like a golden vine,
Flowing softly to the perfect design.
He overcomes problems without any regret,
He's a shining star I will never forget.

Sophie Mapplebeck (14)

THE BUILD

The lorries came first,
All yellow and loud,
Disturbing the villagers who rarely made a sound,
The sheep ran far,
The cattle wide,
But only to fill,
The people with pride.

In each trailer,
A ton of bricks lay,
Waiting patiently for that hour in the day,
The sun shone high,
The workers would sweat,
And the children waited around,
For the beloved cement

The foundations were set,
The entrance blocked,
But never once did the people think to stop,
They ushered them in,
One by one,
Various jobs,
Made to be done

When they started,
The thrill was superb,
Met by the wonderful songs of the birds,
They carried the tools,
In each hand,
Slowly accomplishing
The targets they'd planned

The rooms were made,
Divided by walls,
Made even bigger for the food hall,
The carpet came next,
Rolled out in strips,
They admired their work,
With hands on their hips.

Soon furniture came,
Along with paint,
Making everything seem nice and quaint,
They added the drawers,
And the beds,
Making sure,
The news was spread

Everything was placed,
Around the rooms,
Celebrating under the fabulous moon,
The roof would hold,
Through wind and rain,
Whilst the children danced,
Through the last day

The lorries went first,
Steaming down the road,
Followed by everything else to go,
And then it was done,
As they put down the gnome,
This wasn't a house,
It was a home.

Cailin Michie (13)

PLEASE EXPLAIN WHY I CAN'T SEE ANY SUN

There's always sun over the horizon.
That's what everyone seems to think.
Things are going to get better.
When one door closes another opens.
After all, the glass is always half full, isn't it?

So explain to me,
Why am I sitting alone,
Trying to compress my emotions
And pretend to myself.

Explain to me,
Why my mind is a mess
And no one seems to realise or recognise my hurt.

Explain to me,
Why I think things will just get worse.

Explain,
Why I can't see any sun.

It seems to me that there's this demonic halo of light
Shrouding our perception,
Making us believe in impossible hope.

It seems to me that the saccharine sun's liquid heat
Intoxicates and allures,
Hiding the sobering reality of . . . of . . . of reality.

Please explain why I can't see any sun.

Malika Jumbe (16)

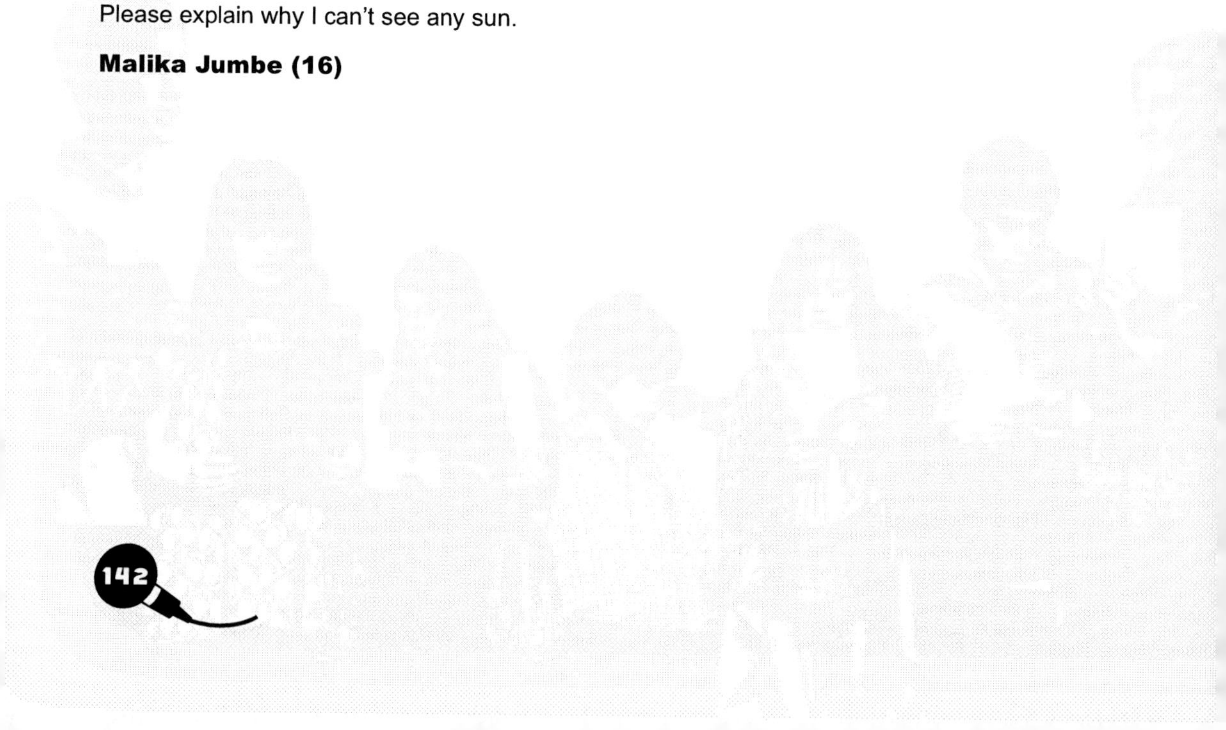

THE WORDS, THEY COME TO ME

I'd like to write a poem but at this moment you see,
Imagination is on holiday and words have deserted me.
My mind is like a block of ice; stops words from getting in,
And still that deadline's creeping closer: my time is wearing thin.
I'd love to come back to the Slam, to feel the swirl of words,
But my words have abandoned me, as hard to catch as birds.
They're fluttering just out of reach, those words so hard to find,
I'm in need of inspiration, something to nourish my mind.
I guess it's emotions I crave, you know, that passionate sort,
For I think that's where most poems come from, a feeling or a thought.
That's just it about poems though: they can't be sold or bought.
For poems are like other art, they're things to love and keep,
Maybe that's why there is writers' block: the words just need their sleep.
For words are living things you know, things that tire and wear out,
And so they need their rest you know, for energy to whizz about,
The words they give their services, the words they give themselves,
To writers and to poets, then they end up in books on shelves.
In books the words are resting, yes, they are sleeping then,
But whenever some new writing's written, they wake up again.
So I guess I can be glad now, for the words have come to me,
But I think that I'll give them a rest now, let them have a break from me.

Molly Coker (13)

HEARTBROKEN

The clouds hurriedly ran away
As the clear blue sky became shrouded
By a thick black mist

All was silent . . .

Until out of nowhere
Sprung a Trident

War was announced!

The ground began to shake and move
Whilst the red walls moved in a circular motion
Opposite to the Earth's crust
Confusion struck upon my face
As the truth spilled to the Earth's surface
By the wide crack in the ground that tore us apart.

Hell was awaiting me,
Ready to swallow me whole
Like a lion ready to pounce upon his prey

I looked for support
But all four red walls crumbled to the ground
Lost in the rubble
I lay emotionless
Because I was heartbroken.

Banusha Rajeenthira (17)

MOONLIT SKY

The night is dark,
The dark means night,
The world is fast asleep,
All the houses - no lights,
All the trees - no movement,
All the animals - shut-eyed,
The only thing living
Is the moon - bright and cheerful.

Ceren Michelle Tüzün (11)

SITTING IN THE DARK WITH A CANDLE IN MY HAND

Sitting in the dark with a candle in my hand,
Illuminated by my thoughts,
Making not a sound,
I slowly tap to the beat of my heart,
I hear a rhythm so strong, and that's when I start,
I have to dance to let my feet be free,
It's just bursting right out, an expression of me,
I hear the tick-tock of the clock
And begin to twirl, feeling the flow of my frock,
I can hear my feet hit the ground,
Feel the music, listen to the sweet sound,
I let my hair loose, it moves in its own way,
An individual being, just knows what it's trying to say,
The beauty of flower petals, with the gorgeous scent,
I don't need choreography to express myself
Or for someone to tell me how it went,
I don't care for opinion, I just feel the need,
To express my little beating heart
That circulates the blood inside of me.

Alicia Horsted (17)

MY DOG SAMMY

S ammy is cooler than a cucumber,
A nd she eats cat food,
M y cat Jiggles is scared of her,
M y cat Keshi likes Sammy a bit,
Y et Sammy steals all of their food.

Joe Williams (9)

A PAWN IN WAR

The bullets were shooting in from all sides,
I couldn't move; I would be killed.
The army planes all around
Signified the start of an endless battle.

Our planes started shooting,
Our opponents standing strong.
They copied us, their bullets
Hitting the side of our planes like knives.

I tried to shoot with them,
But was cast away, seemingly too bad to be part of the action.
At the back, there was nothing to do,
But fly, and stay clear of stray bombs.

Now I would get my revenge,
Not against the British,
But against my own side.
The Germans had angered me.

My plane swooped down,
Below my former allies,
I turned sideways,
Towards the British and their crew.

The British thought I was crazy,
A German pilot, defecting to the other side?
It was unheard of.
They saw me, and started to shoot me down.

The rusted sides of my plane
Started creaking as the bolts were infiltrated,
The windscreen shattered,
Leaving glass weaved into my skin.

As the plane fell down,
Into the sea of blue below,
I looked up at my former comrades,
And cursed them, blaming them for my death.

As far as they were concerned,
I was just a pawn in a huge game of chess.

Kristina Fox (11)

THIS TIME

I don't want you to go,
But I don't want you to stay,
I just wish everything was sorted,
So it didn't end this way.

Every time you leave,
I go out and bring you back,
But every time I do,
You just say you have to pack.

My dream is to dance,
But I can't with you like this,
But you don't really care,
You just give me a goodbye kiss.

Staying up all night crying,
Wondering what to do next,
Whether I should just lie there,
Or just send you a text.

Hoping that it's like the others,
And that you will decide to come back,
But now I've waited too long,
Now it's my turn to pack.

Billi Jo Beach (12)

SPRING

The flowers have come back to say hello,
Say goodbye to all of the snow,
Shorts and skirts are back in fashion,
Can you feel the new year passion?
The children are back out to play,
This is the start to a great spring day,
I've nearly finished my poem now,
These are my last few lines,
Make sure you enjoy spring while it lasts,
Be sure to eat some limes.

Sharday Pratt (12)

DEATH BY LEARNING

Five years of hell,
Five years of misery,
Five years of gutsy work,
Five years of looking at teachers with a smirk.

I'm in Year 7,
Small, scared and frightened,
Working my way up,
Keeping my head down.

Now, I'm in Year 8,
Disliking the Year 7s,
Oh, how I knew how they felt,
But just keep your head down low.

Two years in,
I'm now in Year 9,
Messing around,
Not a care in the world.

Oh dear, Year 10,
That's when we buckle down,
Feeling the pressure,
Feeling the nerves.

Ah, the last year,
11 we go,
I promise not to cry,
But, oh, I just did.

Now, I'm in 6th form,
Feeling just like the Year 7s,
Small, scared and frightened,
Just keep my head down.

For two years later,
Five years of hell really taught me well,
So much achieved,
One step at a time,
Yet I'm still learning,
In this big and scary world,
How to buckle down,
And rule all that to come.

Shama Begum (13)

IT'S THE ANSWER

How can I explain it
When they don't believe it
How can I live with it
When I don't have anyone like me to share it
Is it really worth it,
Living life with a dark shadow over it
With some people you just can't tell them about it.
Some you can but you still can't talk about it.
Some hate people like it.
That's why I have to hide and not act like it
Or when people ask about it
I have to lie and not admit it.
It hurts me having to do it
But I have slowly got through it
So now mainly everyone I know, knows about it.
So even if you don't have a clue about it
You're now going to know it.
I'm a gay boy
Deal with it.

John Edward Robert Dockrill (16)

MY FAMILY

My dad is like a chimpanzee
Who eats bananas all day.
Mum is like a wise owl
Tu-whit tu-wooing all night.
Lee is crazy like a monkey
Swinging from tree to tree.
Kira is like a chatty parrot
Chatting every day.
I am jumpy like a kangaroo
Bouncing around everywhere.

Lucy Gostelow (12)

THE WINTER DAYS

The start of winter was a dull one,
Not very bright.
It's the end of summer,
No late night in sight.

Street lights come on early,
The sun comes up late.
The summer days are over,
Now we have to wait.

Soon it will be colder,
With lots and lots of snow.
When will it fall this year?
Nobody will know.

Dusk will be earlier,
Dawn will be later.
Now we'll have to wait,
Until the end of December.

Once winter starts to end,
The coldness will start to fade.
The frost will no longer occur,
The snow will melt away.

No need for warmth,
No need for extra clothing.
Once the end of winter arrives,
The wasps and bees are awaking.

Insects will have life,
At the very new first dawn.
As winter would've ended,
And creatures would've been born.

Once those cold days have faded away,
Birds will start to chirp and sing.
From then on, we know,
It's the start of spring.

Samuel Lawrence Bateman (14)

MAGIC IS THERE ON THE LEFT

You know reason why the God
Makes our heart
On the left side
Because he knows that we sometimes commit the wrong things
That leads us to the left side of our life
It's because, you will find out the power you had in the left side
Of your life
Because the heart is beating
Makes you believe that you can go right again.

The magic is there on the left
You do wrong, so that you may realise
The magic that lies in the left.

The right path is usually spooky
So you move to the wrong path in the first place
That is the left turn in your life
You get down and then realise
The reason of having the heart at left is also the same

So that you believe and give your life a new name
Starting from the left
Life from the dead
Hope from the broken way

The way that lies in-between your desired destiny
And your present marks
It is just a few steps ahead if you let it out of your heart

The magic is there on the left
You do wrong, so that you may realise
What can be done to your life
To make it right

The magic there on the left.

S Shayan Khalid (14)

AMNESIA

My memories
My life
Myself
Locked behind a door in my head
And I can't find the key.

All I can see is darkness
All I can hear is a slow beeping
My eyes are shut
I open them.

I see the beeping comes from a machine
One of many surrounding me
Behind them, blinding white walls
A hospital?

I look around
Unfamiliar faces surround me
They look down at me, worried
Should I know them?

I look at myself
Tubes feed a liquid into my hand and leg
A plastic mask gives me oxygen
What's happened to me?

A woman begins to speak
I've had an accident, she says
But I'll recover soon
So why does she sound sad?

She continues with tears in her eyes
She says three unfamiliar names
Says they didn't make it
But who are they?

She sees the confusion in my face
She clarifies for me
My mother
My father
My brother
A family I know nothing about

And now I never will

As a tear falls from my face
I remember the time
Only a minute ago
But it feels like an age ago
When all I knew of was darkness
And a slow beeping noise.

Eilis Hafey (14)

HOW CURIOUS!

Inquisitively, admirable, Alice skipped
across the lengthy, chequered hall.
Staring with epic sapphire eyes, the phantasmal cheshire cat
strolled through the vine grasslands.
Like a lion's roar, the Queen of Hearts strictly shouted,
'Off with her head!' on the burnished throne.
As nutty as fruit cake, the erratic Mad Hatter danced
at the tremendous tea party with manic enthusiasm.
Pathetically, the elephantine duchess sang in the wrecked shelter,
which was filled with smashed crockery.
Worrying like a worm when a vicious bird's in sight,
the tardy, white rabbit hurried dramatically
towards the pulchritudinous garden.
Confused, the brawny caterpillar stared in astonishment
at the impeccably behaved child sat on the toadstool.
Bouncing like a space hopper, the irrational March Hare laughed
at puerile jokes next to the epic river.
About to snooze into a splendid slumber,
the comatose dormouse yawned continuously in the china tea pot.
Irate, the fiery jabberwocky defended himself
for the daunting battle was to begin -
but can Alice save Wonderland?

Caitlin Clargo (10)

FATHER'S DAY

F is for Father who is always kind.
A is for angels guarding when you're lost.
T is for tender loving heart.
H is for happy days.
E is for Europe that is calling you.
R is for respect, honesty and kindness.
S is for sharing special moments.

D is for Daddy who is always there for me.
A is for amazing spirit, courage and power.
Y is for yummy, delicious food that you buy for us.

Tewoh-Joy Pessima (9)

LETTING GO

(For Matthew)

I used to believe that we could last forever,
We always said neither one would end it first,
And even though it was such a beautiful love,
It came to an end so suddenly.

I never thought that repeating the same routine day after day,
Would be so precious - you were the only one who made me feel like that,
And I regret how blind I was - never noticing,
That your enthusiasm dwindled against the test of time.

Days pass like the clouds on a windy day, or a dream,
But I know it's reality as I can feel this pain in my heart,
Yet I pretend that nothing ever happened as I get on the train to school,
Although at the same time, all I can think about are the memories we shared.

The metal bench we sat on, holding one another,
The swans we watched on the lake that 'splooged' under the water,
And being self conscious, I always refused to sit on your lap,
Oh how I'd do anything to receive invitations like that now.

Then the time came when it all ended,
My world cast adrift, and everything broken,
Still, I remember how kind you were,
While I sat on the bench crying and holding you tight.

It's funny, how a friendship that becomes something more
Can never truly change back after things don't work out,
Finally, here's something I need you to hear:
I love you so much . . . and I know I always will.

Anna Williams (16)

WHAT MATTERS TO ME

Of all the things I like I guess,
These are the things I like the best,
When work is done and it's time to play,
This is how I spend my day.

With sturdy boots and a heavy sack,
I set off on an uphill track,
Amazing views unfold around,
I pause to take in the sights and sounds,
Singing birds, a glassy lake,
A perfect spot for a well-earned break.

Feeling the wind whip across my face,
Pushing against in a hard-fought race,
Panting, breathless, a rosy smile,
Keep on going, not long till the end,
Laughing along as I cross the finish line,
I'm holding the trophy, feeling very proud.

Time to have some fun and relax,
Playing on the Nintendo, I'm good at that,
Buttons clicking, people cheering me on,
Luigi and Mario whistling,
They're around the track in a lightning flash,
Avoiding bumps and bangs along the way.

Put the cooker on full blast,
Time to make some fruit scones,
Knead, roll, squash,
'Are they ready?' my parents shout,
Get them out of the oven and straight onto a plate,
Cos they're hot, hot, hot!
Shove them into your mouth,
'Oh my gosh! They're amazing!'

Time to go to bed,
No thoughts of work around me,
I'm now cosy and warm,
With my duvet wrapped around me,
A lovely day baking and playing,
Now time to go to sleep,
But first hot chocolate,

It's on its way,
I sip and say, 'Wow!'
I finish my hot chocolate
And fall asleep.

Molly Cronnie (11)

CHRISTMAS!

I wake up and jump out of bed,
Excited my eyes wide,
Looking up and down the hallway,
The snow is falling outside.

Run into my brother's bedroom,
Screaming, 'Wake up, it's Christmas Day!'
Excited I might be,
My brother just says, 'Go away!'

I guess my excitement must be released
On the presents under the tree,
So off I run down the stairs
Thinking of what awaits me.

Beautiful colours and bright lights.
Everything wonderful is within my sights,
All this splendour is giving me an appetite,
For my Christmas dinner which will taste just right.

This is my Christmas and it's clear to see,
This is the most special and best time for me.

Harry Ross (12)

THE WORLD

The sun and blue sky
Time to say bye-bye
In comes the night
Gives you a fright
Everywhere are the mountains
Seas splash like fountains
But stars shining bright
Will keep you alright.

Neelakshi Vasudevan (7)

CORNWALL IS CALLING

Briny, salty sea breeze,
Air fragranced with sea campion,
Sweet sickly ice cream,
Smooth pebbles skidding from under foot,
Glistening rock pools,
Rough ragged rocks just asking to be climbed.
Piping hot fish and chips with extra lashings of vinegar.

Bubbling breakers bombarding the quay,
Gulls squawking,
Tickling sand between my toes,
Skylarks' song on the wind,
Aquamarine ocean,
Sea-polished shells so enchanting to feel,
Clear skies for miles and miles.

Slimy seaweed.
Golden sand,
Perishing sea like ice on bare feet,
Wintry, windswept beaches strewn with seaweed,
Sea sparkling like a pool of glitter glue,
Cornwall is calling . . .

Jasmine Dickson (11)

SEASIDE POEM

At the beach I see the salty and calm sea
I feel the glimmering sun on me
I taste the salty and vinegary chips
I feel the protective suncream on me
I taste the ice cream that children love to eat
I see children splashing in the sea.

Yasmin Dodd (7)

THE SILENCE

The silence of the abandoned building
This place used to be filled with voices,
But then came the virus

It spread quickly
Those who didn't escape in time died.

Now silence rules over this building
The ghostly bodies are pale and white
Almost as if their souls as well as life have been taken

Nobody dares go in here
Not even death

There is no natural light
The only light is from fading strip lights

Then the virus spread
Outside so many died

Now silence rules the earth
The sun was killed by the virus
The only light is coming from dim street lights

The age of Man ended
While the age of silence began.

Hadrian Fletcher (12)

NIDAH KHAN

N idah is a very strong girl, she never gives up on anything
I ntelligence is naturally in Nidah
D ares herself to do stuff
A nd not to forget she's a poet
H ave you ever wanted to laugh till you cry?
Hang out with Nidah, she's a funny girl.

K indly she would do anything in the world to help someone
H appily she would hide her sorrows and smile all the time
A rt? She is best at it
N ow you know everything about her.

Nidah Khan (12)

THE KISS OF THE KNIGHT

Sitting in the streets
With the stars as my covers
And the pavements beneath me as my mattress
I lay here thinking of my past.
How love set me to this path which I am led on now.
My home is crumbling beneath my feet
And my friends turned on me like the night sky
All I have now are the thousands of raindrops kissing my cheek.
The kiss of the night makes me like what is above my covers
And think of something more
Makes me think of hope, maybe of raindrops turning into lips
Stars turning into a blanket
And the pavements turning into the bed I once dreamt upon
But with all the loneliness comes happiness
As my knight in shining armour of my past comes from behind me
Places his hand on my shoulders
A heat struck, travelled down my spine,
Making my emotions spiral out of control
His shadowed head made it impossible to see his eyes once he faced mine.
Never again will my knight kiss me on the lips in a romantic yet desperate way.
The kiss of the knight. My knight
And then he whispered into my ear.
So gentle I did not know until he spoke in his broken voice
Those three final words made it harder to be here.
But worth even more to stay.

Rhian Louise Stowell (15)

FOX

Sly fox
Hunting, staring
Licking, glaring.
Rabbit running
Fox sprinting
Fox pouncing
Rabbit dead.

Lewis Tranmer (9)

EMOTIONS

Emotions, emotions
Happiness should be your daily devotion.
Sadness must go like an erosion
Never to appear as one of your emotions.

If you feel happy, happy, happy
Your days will never feel scrappy.
Happiness is like the roses you smell
And in every text message, you'd like to add 'LOL'.

Why do I feel so sad?
Why do I feel that bad?
I feel so sad I want to cry,
No, there'll be no tear in my eye.

Fear, fear, fear
It has such a leer
Don't worry, I'm not scared. Did you hear?

Emotions, emotions
Happiness should be your daily devotion.
Sadness must go like an erosion.

Michael Lamptey (10)

TAKEN FROM THE LAKE

Once I came across a lake,
that was a very big mistake.
The ripples started to break,
it was like they were going to wake.
I ran, not wanting to be its dinner,
I thought the lake would be the winner.
Coming closer to my feet,
I thought I might also have to meet,
The freezing water closing in,
determined now not to let it win.
A masked figure jumped to my rescue,
all the words I said were, 'Bless you.'
She disappeared into thin air,
the only memory, a golden hair.

Ciara Healy (10)

A GHOSTLY NIGHT

Soon it will be night
A ghost comes to my sight
It gives me a terrible fright
Oh no! What should I do?
Get away from you!

Suddenly it disappears
But I know it's near
As darkness falls
The ghost calls

I feel uptight
I pray to be bright
I feel paranoid
Which makes me annoyed
As I think of a plan
For my life I ran.

Ishika Sakina Haque (13)

LEAVING THE CITY

Hands in pockets, staring at the ground,
Walks a teenage boy not making a sound.
Down his sullen face, hidden by a hood
Falls silent tears, he knew he would,
Have to let out, they'd been welling up inside
Never before like, that had he cried.

He wipes away tears as he walks to the port
He hasn't been spotted, and he hasn't been caught.
He sees the ship, in the sea, all alone,
And realises that it will soon be his home.

Nervously, silently he creeps on board,
There are people in rooms he couldn't afford.
Between two crates, he crouches and stays,
Fresh tears fall as the ship sails away.

Billie Marianne Early (12)

I COULD SAY . . .

I could say my eyes are dry,
Could say that I no longer cry,
But to believe it for a second,
Would just be another lie.

I could say that I don't miss you,
I could tell you I don't care,
But the truth is that I'm broken,
Because you're no longer there.

I could say that I'm okay,
That I never loved you, anyway,
I was not one to jump at shadows,
But for me there is no other way.

I could say a thousand words,
And then add a thousand more,
But unless you're there to listen,
There's no need for them anymore.

I could say that I see clearly,
That look of sadness I despise,
For you make me feel like I'm to blame,
And my sympathy, it dies.

I could say your words burn me,
Like a vial of lethal cyanide,
And when you eventually whisper, 'Sorry,'
It's sad that you're still spewing lies.

Enya Sinead Emma Sharp (14)

ON THE STAGE

She was little and strong
She never did any wrong
Until she made the mistake
Of stepping on the stage.

Everyone was waiting
Anticipating
To see what she would perform
The sweat trickled down
The audience began to frown
This was a mistake
She shouldn't be on the stage!

She opened her mouth
A high note spilled out
So lovely, pure and true
She was amazed
In a daze
Maybe she hadn't made the mistake
Of stepping on the stage after all!

Cheers and smiles
That went on for miles
Shock and excitement
She'd done it!
She'd enticed them!

People now believed in her
They didn't laugh or jeer at her
She was happy
Her dream had come true
But between me and you
She could only sing
As well as she could
Because everything they ever should
Have given her came
'Cause she believed in
Her own type of saviour.

Leanne Katie Cornish (12)

BLACKBERRYS ARE COOL

My new Blackberry is so cool
It's so glam it makes you drool
It is fun to download apps
And find your way with Google maps

BBM is fun to use
Download Adele, GaGa and Muse
My Blackberry is the best
It is not like all the rest

My Blackberry is not old
Change the font italic to bold
Flip-up phones are so old news
My Blackberry is the one to choose.

Fiona Cameron (12)

THE FOX

There's something strange in the air tonight
A tremor running through the trees
And strange mists sweeping stealthily through the park
Witching hour is one hour gone and yet . . .
And yet something lurks beyond my vision
Just an inch from my grasp
And in the gloom of the garden path
Its toes brush the line of moonlight,
Always keeping to the shadows.

Waiting, watching.

Suddenly . . .
A howl, a shriek, the scrambling of paws and the scuffling of claws,
The padding of feet on concrete,

The night visitor has arrived,
And she's waiting to be fed.

Atifa Jiwa (17)

A CRY FOR HELP

Some people in this world are starving,
Only just getting by,
When you see the TV ads,
It makes you want to cry.

There's people that need water,
From very valuable sources,
While others just need homes,
And simply don't have the resources.

You see people dying,
As mothers cry for help,
Their little children are injured,
All they can do is shout and yelp.

Most are in war-torn countries,
Scary places to live,
Just a donation every month,
That's all you have to give.

Some children get neglected,
Their parents don't have the money,
To care for their child's needs,
It really isn't funny.

Not knowing where to get a meal,
They've never been to school,
Most of us turn our heads away,
It really isn't cool.

Most of these poor people die,
Innocent souls ascend to above,
If more people like us gave,
They'd find help, but most of all love.

Charlotte Eleanor Lucy Mellor (13)

I AM

Expect the unexpected as you live
In murals painted by a manipulative.
Hear of those who are truly disrespected.
Open up! So you'll not be disconnected.

I am God who dominates beyond Earth.
I am the mysteries of your nightmares.
I am the arrival of a new birth.
I am that crimson vicious hand who tears

Away the justice of this joyful life.
I am soft silk of a sweet silent rape.
I am the youthful stabbing of a knife.
I am the abused, veiled with a mouth tape.

I am the sorrowful droplets of a child.
I am mint greed, gulped by the drunken West,
Who craves over the value of this wild world,
That has turned away from the voicelessness.

I am the magnificent art of con.
I am a torn book open for education.
I am that playful, business selling don.
I am technology changing in civilisation.

I am the prelude of a ridiculous war.
I am that terrorist who blew up a world full of innocent flowers.
I am a soldier who fought for nothing, no more.
I am death at every door, every minute of every hour.

I am lost between the past and present.
I am a glorious landscape that will soon turn to dust,
A thing we cannot move from these events that are unpleasant.
I am what everybody has destroyed. Trust.

Turn that luxurious world over,
Everything withers like a dead rose.
Screaming, dying, shooting is your first hangover.
Chaos' are the hailstones of your weeping woes.

I am killed every day:
War, droughts, poverty is what I exist through.
This dream I dream has no such pathway.
The hearts of many beat like a heartless drum.

I am the reflection of what the world sees today.
I am that person who runs away
From the people who suffer a tear,
I am fear.

Dinah Mehnaz Ali (15)

HIM

He looked at me often,
His blue eyes staring into my soul.

He hugged me when I needed warmth,
His body protected me from the outside world.

He held my hand when no one looked,
His fingers entwined with mine.

He gave me my first kiss,
His lips soft and gentle.

He called me beautiful no matter how I looked,
His smile reassured me.

He told me he wanted to be with me,
His voice made it sound so believable.

He said he loved me,
He lied.

Emma Jayne Drinkwater (15)

IMMERSION IN EMOTION

Like God, there is in Man, a darker mind,
That sits behind the rational countenance,
And broods on deep abolished thoughts;
Where aimless rivers of black pitchy tar
Wind like serpents, down into the core,
And merge in boiling lakes of frothy bile,
That suffocates the breath with choking fumes.
And deep within the broiling bubbling lake,
Made fat and gorged with constant fuel of hate,
The horrid, gross reflection in the mire
Of Man's own filthy dark desires . . .

Joseph Sale (17)

OUR OWN LITTLE WORLD

How many worlds can you find?
There's thousands out there
In the atmosphere
Maybe here we could find our own little place
That looks like a face
And has a little grace
But what about mistakes?
It has to be perfect
No matter what
Just like the thousands
In the atmosphere
So here we will find our little place
And it will look like a face
And it will definitely have grace
Because it's our own little place.

Jessica Tonks (14)

LOVE, HOW IT HURTS

You're crying again, yet the tears aren't from being sad,
They are probably from the ending words that we just had,
Said you want to be alone, but your presence will never leave my home,
And as you walked out the door, I had never felt my soul that weak before,

My heart burns and my brain has run dry,
Thought this love could never die,
I'm holding on to nothing,
When I should of had something,
I never listened, so I never learnt,
That's why goodbye was the last word I ever heard.

Brandon Webb (15)

DEAR TRUE LOVE (THE HIGHWAYMAN)

The midnight moon came shining too soon,
The horse was galloping fast,
My love for you was strong and fearless,
My heart was burnt like brass.
The jewels you gave me
Surrounded my heart,
The tail and the mighty marks,
My death was yours,
Your death was mine,
King George's men drew the fine line.
The highwayman came
Riding down the gypsy highway,
Over the purple moor,
The highwayman came
Riding silently, breaking my heart.
The twinkle in your eye,
The way you kissed goodbye,
The way our lips touched,
Oh I miss you very much.

My life is not worth living,
If you're not by my side,
The gypsy highway's worthless
If I can't be your bride.

Georgia Spiteri (13)

RAINBOWS

The rainbow stretches its body across empty valleys,
Tickling the sky as it goes.
Beaming at the tender grass below, its misty rays shine,
Lighting the way for animals who look up,
Blinded by its beauty.
Its colours are jewels,
Each delicate and unique in their own way,
Reflecting off the deep waters of the sea,
Singing a silent song to the creatures of the water.
The rainbow makes dark forests spring to life,
Giving them a magical atmosphere,
Making the trees dance and the grass sway
To the rhythm of the soft breeze.
Believe it or not, rainbows truly are magical.

Catherine Henslowe (11)

MESSAGE TO THE MOON

I am sending a message to the moon,
I wonder if aliens will read it soon.
See my message ride through the sky,
I give it a wave and say goodbye
When my message reaches the moon in a year,
I will be able to hear:
Aliens say,
'This message is really good,
I must visit Earth if I should.'
I am sending a message to the moon in a day or two,
I wonder if aliens look like me or you?

Charlotte Harrison (12)

THE MONSTER YOU'VE BECOME

I've got a picture of us etching my name in the sand
Now you run around with a loaded gun in your hand.
Said it's for protection and what doesn't kill you, makes you stronger
But Mummy's been crying a lot, she can't wait any longer.
I'm only a young girl trying to understand this crazy world
But this destruction you cause people's lives is difficult to bare.
The children are scared, they were not prepared.
Not prepared to see their father die
Or their mother scratch her blood-splattered face and cry.
Bottled up their thoughts in their young minds,
Frightened to speak, they just sit there and hide.
Hoping the mad men will only pass by this time.
They wonder why these men are here,
Putting them through hell. They're constantly living in fear.
Their innocence is wrestled down,
As they listen to their sister pound the ground with her tiny fists,
As the savage man grabs her wrists.
You're high and you're p****d.
No matter how hard she tries she can't resist.
There's blood on the floor, you're happy and want some more,
But she can't stand this life anymore.
Your b*****d child she bore.
Found a bullet with her name on it,
Shot it in her mouth and choked on it.

Asma Shatwan (17)

THE WAR FLOWER

A sign, a gift, a remembrance and beauty,
Your past, your present or maybe your duty,
As you walk through knolls, a sea of red,
They catch your dreams when you're tucked up in bed,

A flicker, a glance, a wish or hope,
They attract your eyes but some cannot cope,
The tip of life, splendour and courage,
Stream in a sea of beautiful poppies,

The last post sings o'er the land,
Remains of courage in Normandy's sand,
The deep red symbolises the blood which was shed,
But they still grew over the English dead,

Wheat turns soft and glimpses of red
appear and poke out their little heads,
Skylarks and thrushes swoop and dive,
But the remembrance of war is still alive,

They gradually fall, disappear and die,
Until there are only a few to catch your eye,
In time there are only a few specks left
And one by one a piece of soul is bereft,

Let's not forget those to fall,
But just to remember their willing call,
Their vibrant colour, life and harm,
For with the change, comes a new dawn.

Evie Courtier (14)

HELLO, SUMMER

She looks down at me every day.
Her bright eyes absorb the green grass.
Her forty degree rays pound,
Over the sea, as the wind does pass.

Her shimmering smile appears at last,
Only to attract the bikinis.
She ripens the coconuts and mangoes,
And heats the ice cold Martinis.

She watched so very proudly,
As the little baby lay,
Reminiscing her adoring eyes
On this fine beautiful day.

Girl and boy; hand in hand
Sharing a delightful kiss.
They look right up at her,
Eyes glimmering with bliss.

Parked on the bench, a grey old man
Looking up at her smile
Passionate, fruitful
Careful!
She only lasts a while.

Miren Hare (15)

THE MESSAGE TO MYSELF

The beat of a drum,
The scream of a lung,
The beat of my heart, it's what keeps us apart,
I want to respect, the dearly depart,
But I look to the future, utmost anticipated
In the recess of my mind,
I carry one thought, belated
'To go back to the start' and tell myself 'I made it'.

Jawed Khalifa (17)

PROGRESSION

Without the dreamer,
There is no life,
Without the logic,
There is always strife.
Without the path,
The future is unattainable,
As without the legs,
The table is unstable.
But may it also be so,
That the crutch be futile,
Without the broken arm or leg,
And remain unused and in a pile,
The confines of convention,
Taken down a peg.
And so it is true,
The recipe is invalid,
Without ingredients on cue,
Our lives are grey and pallid.
So let the dreamer dream,
And let the logic instruct,
Let the future have a path,
Free of those who obstruct.
Let the entrepreneurs,
Add the common sense,
And the medicinal cures,
Provide a healing trend,
Let the work of others,
Guide you to yours,
But make it count, make it worth,
More than the persons before.

Neha Din (14)

I'M NOT MUCH OF A POET

I wish that I could write poetry.
From the crash of a wave at high tide
To the tiniest waver of a buttercup's petal,
From the creak of a weight-stricken floorboard
To the constant vibrations of the hummingbird's wing,
Captured in words like a picture without paint.
Or maybe just with paint that we can't see
Without the canvas of our impossible thoughts.

I wish that I could write poetry,
Then I could tell you about the taste
Of the most divine food, that through anything else
Would be simply indescribable,
How it dances and blossoms like a delicate flower
Across your long-awaiting taste buds.

Or maybe, I could tell you about
The horrors of our cruellest world
Like bonds frayed and snared
Between lovers, families, friends
By forces beyond our control.
Blood shed needlessly
That stains the ground scarlet
Whilst the old man laughs and rubs his hands with glee.

Or I could tell you about the injustice
Or poverty, disease, corruption
That taints our perfect world
Like a blot streaked across the canvas.
Or maybe, that's what makes us beautiful . . .
Imperfections are unique, and set us apart,
Like an abstract composition
We are a masterpiece.

But unfortunately, I can't
Because I'm really not much of a poet.

That's not to say I never tried.
I sat down at my desk and willed my mind
To compose like Beethoven
Or paint like Monet
Or dance, or sing
Anything!
But it stubbornly refused.

I strained every sinew
And broke the paintbrush of my thoughts
And poked my mind's eye by accident.

Compositions misted by an angry haze
And blotted by tears.
I have the most potent emotions,
But they stubbornly refuse
To showcase themselves in ink.

Eventually, I put down my quill.
I guess I'm not gifted
But if we were all special,
Nobody would be!

I hope you see a mirror in these words
Of crumpling paper
And ripping my hair out
And screaming at shadows
Can you see your reflection?
Or are you just too lucky?

Oh genie, if you ever did exist,
Can I please have my three wishes now?
To be whisked into a different land
Or summoned to the juror's court
Or Satan's fiery Hell.
Anything but to be seated here!
Anything!

So, I sat myself down
And realised the most important thing.

Imperfections
Are perfect in their uniqueness and originality.

So, I'm not much of a poet,
But I hope my efforts bear fruit.
Irony laces my ire-filled words
With a sprinkle of tears
And a dash of imagination
My recipe's completed.

So, I proclaim with a smile
And a great deal of undeserving pride;

I'm not much of a poet,
Isn't it beautiful?

Daniella Cugini (13)

YOUR SHADOW WILL NEVER CHANGE YOU . . .

She is your shadow both day and night.
The nearing future can never be truly in sight.
You never know what may happen;
As she flows through your element all the time.

God, has given her presence to you; as a 'gift',
With the scarring restlessness you must deal with.
She makes you, who you are,
But . . . will she ever go away?
Perhaps just for one day?

Like an enemy, she never warns you when she'll haunt.
She does not inform you when she will come.
The unquenchable thirst, and exhaustion she brings.
But only you know her for real . . .

The invasion she brings into your life,
With the fear and gloom you often feel.
The price you pay for one simple mistake;
Forces you to take action
Through your llllooooonnnngggg journey with her . . .

Why me? is cried more often than not.
With the unsteadiness and tiredness you repeatedly deal,
And the overwrought emotion: now a part of your life
But you know that God has designed her for a specific purpose.

It is not clear how long she will be here, therefore:
She provides you hurt,
She provides you anxiety,
She provides despair,

Nevertheless . . .

She makes you stronger through all of the hurt,
She makes you realise how lucky you are,
She may one day leave you,
And your hopes and dreams can commence,
But until then . . .
Your shadow will never change you . . .

Sarah Ann Mather (17)

SIX MONTHS HAS COME AND GONE

It's a mystery to why you went
You left my heart misshaped and bent
I understand it was the end to your pain
But the beginning to your fame

Six months has come and gone
You're Nan, my number one
Sometimes I just wish you were here
To hold me and save me from my fear
You'd tell me to chase my dreams
You'd say I was as bright as light beams

You were like my second mom
But your time was ticking like an unstoppable bomb
We knew the end was near
I tried so hard not to shed a tear
I just wish you could see me grow
But a week before Christmas you went with the snow
You said your goodbyes
Then slowly closed your eyes

Six months has come and gone
You're my nan, my number one
I miss you
I love you.

Fallon Naylor (14)

MRS CHAPWICK'S IN A MOOD TODAY

Don't slouch on your chair
Don't tap your feet
Don't comb your hair
Keep quiet!
Mrs Chapwick's in a mood today.

I don't know what's got into her today
Is someone parking in her space?
Or is Jessy making a face?
Or is it that she needs a cry?

Chiquita Simpson Martin (9)

MEMORIES OF AN ALZHEIMER'S SUFFERER

It seems to me that certain words are tossed around so carelessly these days,
That we forget their true meaning.
Words like 'true love', 'perfection', and my personal favourite:
'Unforgettable'.

'I'm sorry . . . what was the question?'

Perhaps a better suited word is 'memorable'. For I always forget
What I'm meant to remember, but
Sometimes long-forgotten things come back to me, like boomerangs,
Or birds in summer.

'Do I remember? Some things . . . Sometimes . . .'

I remember Her. I remember Her name . . . well I don't
But it sounded soft, like the first rays of sunshine
On freshly mown grass, and it rolled off my tongue,
Like a song I've always known.

But what is it? It's on the tip of my tongue . . .

I remember those days . . . well, sort of . . .
I believe there was a wedding once.
But all that's left is the rustle of white satin,
Punctuated only by two voices
That murmured 'I do.'

'It's funny how some things stay with you . . .'

I remember those nights . . . secluded from the world we'd sit,
Bathed in the red glow of the lamplight, and talk about anything.
But now the room is hazy, and the topics of our discussions
Seem to slip my mind.

'Though it worries me sometimes . . . it's strange . . .'

Sometimes, it's as though I'm seeing these things for the first time.
It's almost like they're someone else's memories,
Or parts of a silent movie I can't remember.
Sometimes it's as though I was never there at all.

'But I'd remember that face . . . that face is unforgettable.'

And he smiled blankly, distracted by forgotten yesterdays,
Into eyes full of tears, that rolled slowly down
That unforgettable face.
And She reminded Herself that he'd love Her
If he could remember Her.

It seems to me that certain words are tossed around so carelessly these days,
That we forget their true meaning.
Words like 'true love', 'perfection', and my personal favourite:
'Unforgettable'.

Sarah Parker (17)

DREADING IT . . .

School was always the same,
It always had been.
But it still came dreading
When I was young.

The journey to the bus,
Was a very long drag,
It lasted forever,
In utter silence.

They'd laugh and call me names,
As if I was deaf,
Shouting it to the world
That I was big, fat.

On the bus, even worse,
The songs they would sing
Echoing in my head,
Ringing in my ears.

Then lessons came along,
Not my fault I knew
All the correct answers
And was star student.

All the teachers loved me
But the days grew long,
With them bickering long,
Driving me insane.

It finally ended,
But didn't stop there,
There were many hours
Of abuse via text.

I would hardly use
My phone and laptop,
Afraid to do work online
Scared to do anything.

Soon no one liked me,
My mum, my dad, my gran,
The teachers hated me,
I now know nothing.

I've ended up alone
Because I didn't tell,
It never got sorted out,
It grew worse and worse.

Those people don't annoy
Anyone anymore,
We've all grown up now,
We've all got our jobs.

I always wanted to be
A doctor or a nurse
But I never got the grades
Because they got in my way.

They all got their dream jobs
But I'm stuck as a cashier,
Counting the money all day
All night eating toast.

I saw a girl from high school
She said, 'How's your life?'
I merely said to her,
'I'm not who I used to be.'

I never sorted out
The bullying I had,
It will get worse and worse
And then you can't put it right.

Megan Dunstan (12)

BREATHING UNDERWATER

I make my way across the beach,
My bare feet skim the sand.
My eyes are shining from the tears,
I clutch seashells in my hand.
I untie my hair, wind whipping my cheeks
And then I start to wait.
But you're never coming and you never will
Because I'm already far too late.

It's been a year since you died.
Stolen away by the icy tide
To a place where people don't come back
So why am I even here?

All I see is sparkling blue,
The frothy waves that enticed you.
Staring like I'm in a dream
I drift to the end of the pier.

I outstretch my arm nearer the seas.
I'm closer to water than land.
The ocean flows away from me,
The shells drop out of my hand.
And then the tide comes in again
And washes away my fears.
Then I jump . . .
And I'll be with you
Until the last shell disappears . . .

Alice Walton (13)

WHAT INSPIRES ME

What inspires me is music,
It's there when I'm sad, happy or sick,
It can be club, pop, grime or classic,
Or one that doesn't make so much racket.

What inspires me are my good friends
Because they've got my back,
When they need me I won't slack,
We keep together like a train track,
We are as a boiled egg with no crack.

What inspires me is my family
Because they always love me.

Denzel Eze Simpson Martin (12)

MY DAD INSPIRES ME

My dad inspires me,
because he is always there for me,
he makes the world a better place.

When he is with me,
he makes me feel safe.
My dad looks after me,
to make sure I'm happy,
he is never snappy.

My dad is so kind
to everyone that walks by.
You can never find a dad
like mine.

Alana Simpson Martin (10)

LOB DAMAN IN SEA

The pitter-patter
(Of hidden stalkers' yearnings)
Itch victims' dark hearts.

Actions have rippled across the land,
Whistling in the stark sand
Of blood,
Blood that tastes like dirt on my shrivelled conscience,
Like syrup,
Sweet.
I've forgotten feelings,
They're weak,
Too strong.

Smartened uniforms
(Smeared with triumph polish)
Clench skin in the rain.

Tears burrow the golden dirt,
Tears and sorrow is what makes some hurt.
The cactus prickles in the window,
Grunting for help.
The people grow motionlessly in the garden,
Waiting for the men's pardon,
Polishing their uniforms in the rain.
My son and two wives - going down the drain.

A beaten track,
Wanders to a house of god(s)
(People squat inside)

The clip-clap of their feet,
Rains down on the harshness of my breath,
We're hiding in our sympathy,
Until there's nothing left,
Each snatch of conversation,
Is a convulsion of my imagination,
Sprinting from my vessels,
Permanently unsettled,
Is adrenaline of lost life . . .

Doors open only,
When waited on patiently,
To those who knock (ask).

Before,
They had a leader -
Without a cause,
Before
They had to leave him -
Without applause.
I rose up,
Out of the cinders surrounding.
I rose up,
And they needed a crowning.
I stopped all the fighting,
The terror,
The rape.
I stopped their heads popping,
They were popping - like grapes.
I chopped up some freedom,
And served it with faith,
And dazzled them with eternity,
And it tasted great.
Like syrup,
Sweet.

Fear is the spice of souls,
(Only cowards need more salt)
Lusting bravery.

At f(th)irst there was nothing,
My vision grew, still sings.
But then cancer came,
Un-holstered their guns:
And we were leprosy - on the run,
Hated by everyone,
Shunned by the rest,
The voice of the people?
I was a pest.
So we showed our faces,
And flexed our strength,
And before I forgot it,
Our currency was death.

Weapons when ready
(Baying for the caress of death)
Are holstered by guns.

I think of a microscope,
And watch my life length,
I spit on a cockroach,
And lose all my strength.
A nothing descends,
Smiling the end,
I look at my corpse bag,
My body is spent.

Silence creeps through,
Emptiness is only here,
To bear bait violence

Strength,
The strength to think?
Knock
Yes
The strength to fight?
Knock
Yes
The strength that's right?
Yes . . .
Smack!
No.

'Get down, get up, get on the floor'
'Don't freakin' think of it - I'm watching the door'
I take up my shield,
'Just shoot his wife'
Bang!
'No mate, no mate, I can't take his life'
'If you won't I will'
I will with this knife.
'I got him, I got him - it was me'
What do we do?

'Lob da man in sea,
It's in your name - Osama:
Bin Laden is dead.'

Alfie Green (15)

AM I NORMAL YET?

Wired on a rush as high as the sky
and, don't you dare knock me down,
because today I could eat the whole wide world.
But
never forget the way I crashed and burned
a city burned down in the flame of my eyes
and I am hung on a wire, halfway between my
conscience and my neck.

They gave me a prescription,
just to make sure,
(I swear I was only slightly psychotic
at the time.)
But . . .

Next day:
I am trying to concentrate on . . . wait, what?
Whilst leaves curl and spin like tiny dancers,
connected to each other, intertwining dreams,
the movements of something higher.
There's a panther in the garden,
only it's much smaller,
and its eyes are like emeralds.
It slinks with discs in the spine rising, falling,
spaced like the rungs of a ladder.
I sort of think:
maybe I should kill it?
Forget pills.
I'm God.

Rachel Michaella Finn (17)

WAR LIFE

As the last shot fired
As the last bomb blazed
I walked outside full of rage.
As it was the cold dead of night
Every soldier was out of sight
Though I was aware
I would jump if a soldier was to scare.
My family gone
Though not dead
I still remember them sitting at the edge of their beds.
Old enough to not share a tear
I swore under my breath
Before I disappeared.

Rominique Raphael Makuba (12)

THE CINEMA

I am big but can be small,
But firstly, need to be installed.
For people to come and adore me,
After paying just a small fee.

Lights go out, my room is dark,
My clothes are stripped, people start to lark.
As a bright light starts to shine out of me,
The people are quiet, finally.

I illustrate all day, I illustrate all night,
Sometimes I show romance,
Sometimes I show fight.
However soon I am penned,
In a place where I cannot transcend.

My daily routine is just like this,
where I am expected not to remiss.
As people leave, people go,
as I wait for another day when I must, again show.

Zainab Raza Bukhari (13)

MY BROKEN HEART

My day starts with you,
My day ends with you,
This is no lie,
It is true!

You are the one in my dreams,
You are the one near me,
You and I are . . .
Like water in a stream.

You are my song,
I am your tune,
Together we make love,
That lasts for long.

I still smile,
When I remember the time,
In school you looked into my eye,
While walking home a mile.

We had our hands in hand,
When we danced in that party,
Remember the song?
It was our favourite band!

'I love you!' you said,
To make my day,
But why did you change your mind?
Later you made me sad!

You left me on that day,
On my birthday,
I curse that day,
When you went away!

My day started with you,
My day ended with you,
This was no lie,
It was true!

Ruhi Shah (12)

THE SHADOW IN THE DOORWAY

I see a shadow in the door,
Its form is vague, its image blurs,
But though I cannot hear its voice,
Something deep inside me stirs.

I up and arise, from demi-slumber,
Tossing the sheets back onto the bed,
And with my eyes half-filled with wonder,
I climb through the window: the streets are dead.

No voices stir to break the hallowed
Silence of the still-born gloam,
The shadow glides beside me, and,
In this wasteland, my soul does roam.

The liquid or of grim-faced streetlamps,
Lights, before me, a golden road.
The same path, now dull and monotonous,
Where this land's kings and queens once strode.

The glory of the empire so boundless,
That it once held the world in its little white glove,
Reduced to nought but endless grey,
Now scattered, out, to the skies above.

I turn to my guide, that errant figure,
And it takes on a truer shape,
I see indistinct, a male form,
Half-hid beneath the billowing cape.

The shadow coalesces, I see its true body,
A man clad in mud-splattered green.
He wears about him an overcoat,
Through it, his wounds are clearly seen.

'Dulce et Decorum' the drill sergeant said,
As he sent us on out to war.
'This one'll break the Huns, laddy,
After this, there will be no more.'

We are the youth who died like cattle,
Our blood shed for this place, this land.
But they sold us out, the leaders,
To shape it with their own hand.

What honour rests now in this place,
Where the ruthless and vicious is king?
What beauty and grace in the streets,
Where purpose is everything?

They stripped the pride of this place,
This isle, once so tall, so proud.
These roads, where I too once walked,
Are under a terrible shroud.

You, my friend, are not of this land,
But bear this message well,
For if you cannot stop the slide,
This place is sure destined for Hell.

Take up your glorious mantle, Britons,
Amongst your fellow men!
Let the sounds of Britain,
Ring out, ring out again!
Lest the politicians and the liars,
They lead you far astray,
Recite to yourself these words again and again,
And you'll never lose your way.
We fought the Huns in World War One,
We stopped the Nazi fiend,
But this death of identity,
Is the gravest threat I have ever seen.
Take up the arms of pride, then, friends,
Let Arthur's banner unfold!
Never forget your past,
And let your heart be bold!

Siddharth Venkataramakrishnan (17)

LIFE WITH A LOVING MUM AND DAD

From the moment you were brought into the world
Your life had begun.
Your first smile, warmed your parents' hearts,
Your first words, made them cry happy tears,
And your first footsteps made them so proud.
From when your attitude came,
It made your mum and dad smile,
And your behaviour, well let's not talk about that part!
When you're in the teen years, you seem to be in more trouble,
But your mum and dad still love you,
Even though they might be a bit cross with you.
You pass through school and university
And you get really, really good grades,
And your mum and dad, are so glad that you're just their kid.
When you find someone you love and you eventually get married,
Your parents show you and your newly wed husband,
Some photos of you, when you were a kid, in your head,
You say you can't believe your mum and dad just did that!
As your life carries on, you and your husband
Have your very own children
And you do, what your parents did to you,
Which was to just love them and do anything for them.
As you look back, which you will do,
You think of two special people,
Two people that made your life happy,
Unique and a joy to live;
And that's your mum and dad!

Maggie Barrow (14)

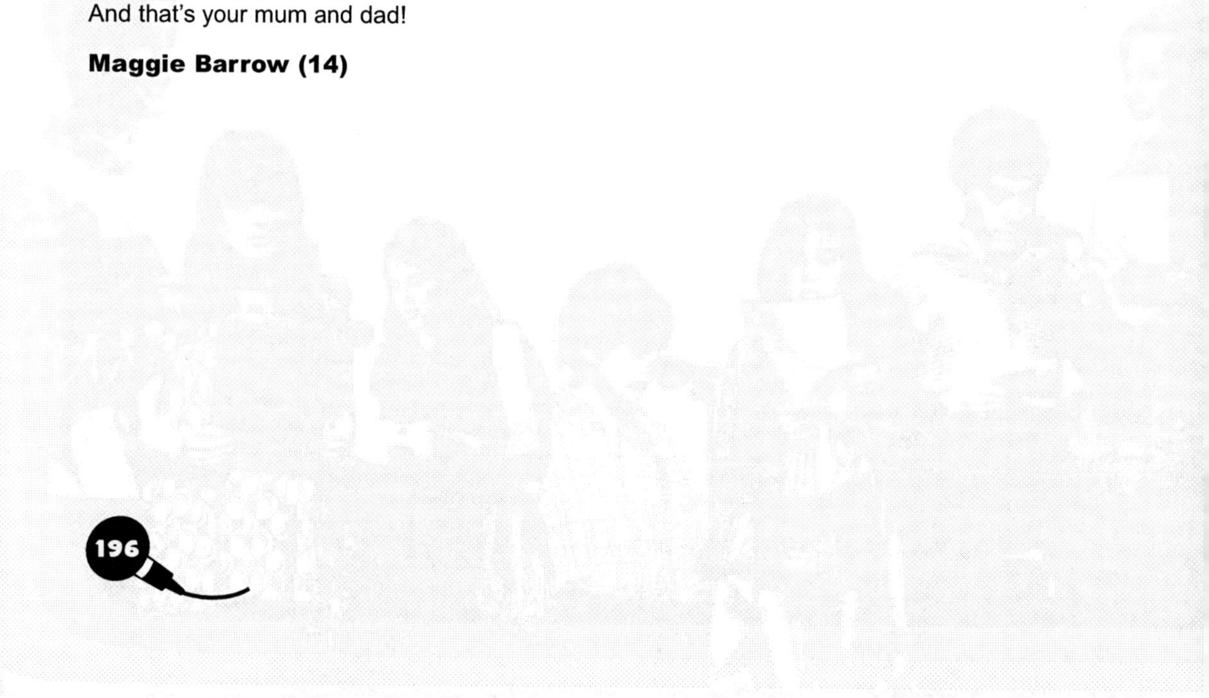

THE SILENCE

There is silence in the cinema,
There is silence in the library,
There is silence when I'm playing in the yard,
Wherever I play there's always silence.

I held my tongue and didn't speak
While I watched a rabbit hop,
I held my breath and didn't touch
As I watched a beautiful butterfly,
I only touched, I didn't speak,
My rabbit, cute and sweet.

There is silence in the world
Where people only relax not speak,
There is silence up in Heaven
Where people's spirits lay,
There is silence where I lay asleep
When the world is dark.

Jade Bagley (12)

RUBY

She wags her tail when running to greet us,
her floppy ears and twitchy nose, her tongue that licks us.
She loves her tennis ball that we throw for her.
When it comes to breakfast, dinner and tea
her crunchy biscuits and chewy sticks are the best for our Ruby.
Ruby runs free when off her lead,
enjoying her walks in the fields around.
At night she sleeps in her comfy bed
all curled up till it's time to wake up!

Connor Garnett (11)

YOU WOULD HAVE LIKED IT HERE

The freshly cut grass, smells sweet in the air,
The birds sing in the trees,
And as I sit, I can't help but think,
That you would have liked it here.

The snowdrops bloom along the side of the road,
So fragile, white as pearls,
And as I look, I can't help but know,
That you would have liked it here.

The cold winter snow, falls and covers the world,
Like a soft, white blanket,
And as it settles, I can't help but wonder,
That you would have liked it here.

The sun has come out, and the flowers have bloomed,
A rainbow of colourful petals,
And as I admire them, I can't help but be certain,
That you would have liked it here.

If you were here, I know you'd have loved it,
The beauty that reminds me of you,
But all I can do, is just be sure,
That you *would* have liked it here.

Ashleigh Messenger (13)

WEAKLING

Dawn fledgling flutters defiantly
Through a fury of splitted outcry.
Weakling pecked at,
Pushing to the tip of an elevated branch
Leaning collected
Amazed at the world beneath:
Beaded dreary sculptures
sending dizzy bewilderment.
'Weakling' takes an animated spring
to dominate the sky.

Amy Hodgkins (16)

MY BOX OF SPECIAL ITEMS

My box of special items holds all things,
from princes' crowns to diamond rings.
It's made out of silver and gold
and the hinges made of ice so cold.

If you take a peep inside,
you'll find the things I'd need to hide.
Like my final day at primary school
or the predator in the grass;
so silently they crawl.

I also have the day that my primary school begun,
and the faces of my friends and I
having so much fun.
The drumming of the music playing loud and clear,
and the snow-white frosting of an ice-cold beer.

This box I hide underneath my bed
and guarded by a guard dog with fur so red.
And all the items that you find
are all picked by angels and taken from my mind.

Grace Leighton (11)

THE SEASIDE

Seagulls flying up in the air,
People playing here and there.
Crabs crawl along in the water,
Sun cream on, it's getting hotter!
Looking around the beach for shells,
Ice cream comes with musical bells.
Dolphins splashing in the sea,
There isn't a place I'd rather be!

Jaden Gorazdowski (6)

TREES

A tree is living,
A tree is joy,
A tree is wild,
Colourful,
The leaves are bright,
Orange, brown, green and yellow,
Dancing to the wind,
Talking to birds and things,
A home to the woodland,
A tree can be big, small, fat or slim,
A tree can be all different things,
A tree ages through time, growing, growing, ever strong,
Different types bearing fruits or flowers,
Cherry, peach, plum - how nice,
There are trees that stay green
And don't lose all their leaves every year,
Others go bare without any care,
So look at a tree, be careful of what you see.

Seema Bhela (11)

CLIFF CLIMBING IN WALES

Suspended from a wall of rock,
Hold only by your mere hands,
Towering above the swishing sands,
In the heat of midday.

The hard rock jagged and grey,
Like an assault course at the end of a day,
Thick with slime and barnacles,
Leathered with clumps of seaweed,
In the heat of midday.

Destroyed by the pounding water,
As if in the middle of a massive slaughter,
Tethered to this giant wall,
While making your gruelling ascent,
In the heat of midday.

Ben Caro (12)

LOOK AT OUR WORLD

People's joys may be money,
People's pride may be their looks,
People's happiness may be their phones,
But do they think about the world?

Life and peace is at crisis,
It is not too late to make a change,
It lies without our fate.
In this world black hearts go to war,
There is no love anymore.
You tell me, what do you see?
A big glory grin or a face full of sin.
Turn to the people next to you,
Do you know what they've been through?
Look deep in their eyes,
Has it been all clear blue skies?
People's joys may be money,
People's pride maybe their looks,
People's happiness may be phones
But do they think about the world?
Life and peace is at stake,
This chance we must take.
Everyone thinks they have joy, pride and happiness,
But they are missing love.

Priyanka Karsan (12)

WILL I GET THROUGH?

I don't come from the richest country in the world
And shop at the latest stores,
I am who I am and I am not what I am not,
Let me be.

Life sometimes is a struggle for me but I will get through.
Pain is my friend and poverty is my neighbour . . .
Does that mean I won't survive?
I see people with fancy cars and big houses
And when they see me they stare
And their eyes talk so loud, 'Look at the nuisance.'

Disgrace is my wife and my struggle is my child,
We are one happy family
We never leave each other's side,
Is this love worth the crime?
Should I cry or smile? Is this going to end or forever continue?
Should I keep raising my head high . . . will I get through?

Death is my sudden option, confusion is haunting.
'Is there something you would like to share before you disappear?'
A sudden voice I hear.

Fear is near, will I get through?
And my heart starts to come clear with a voice worth an ear,
Will I get through?

I will get through.

Thandeka Moyo (15)

I LOVE MY CAT

I rresistible

L oving
O riginal
V ery, very happy
E ver so special

M y baby
Y ou're the best

C uddly
A lways playful
T igger.

Shannon Gorazdowski (9)

MYSTERIOUS WORLD

I live in an indescribable moment of trust and possibility.
In a whisper of worries, comfort lies within the simplest fear.
I, the giver of happiness follow the blue sky
To a warming giggle and playful joy.
Only when the world is together and can feel peace
Will hope shine through song and pure soul.
Beneath the stars of trust lies love.
Believe in your own mysterious world
And bring trust and laughter into your own life.

Ellen Jones (11)

A FRIEND LIKE YOU!

I love you lots, like Jelly Tots
I love you move, than getting on the dance floor
You're lovely, great and my best mate
I will always be there, because I care

Tonight, a flower may die
The sun may set
But a friend like you
I'll never forget!

Your name is precious
It will never grow old
It's engraved in my heart
In letters of gold!

You're funny, caring, and crazy as heck
Sweet, beautiful, and you're bigger than a speck

Today someone asked me if I liked you
I laughed, I said, 'Haa! That's funny
Because I flipping love you to bits!'

A friend like you I'll never forget
A friend like you I'll love forever
A friend like you is more than amazing
A friend like you and me should forever be together!

Aislin Marr (12)

OVER PROTECTIVE

Doesn't let me hang out with my friends when I feel like it.
Doesn't let me decide what I want to wear.
Doesn't let me eat what I want to eat.
Doesn't let me go where I want to go.

Doesn't let me do what I want to do.
Doesn't let me talk to who I want to talk to.
Doesn't let me have any fun when I would like to.
Doesn't let me be free.

She loves me more than I want her to
And I love her, my mum.

Abirami Karunatharan (13)

A LESSON TO BE LEARNT

She wanted to be a hero
But really she was a fool
Because she was a little girl
Who messed about at school
She didn't try in lessons
Her homework was never done
All she really wanted
Was to mess about and have fun
The years quickly passed
And her days at school were over
All her friends have good jobs
But she struggled to stay sober
She couldn't say no to the drugs
Nor the pressure from the local thugs
At sixteen she had a baby
Is this really the life
That both her parents wished for?
Perhaps if she had tried at school
Then things would be different . . . maybe.

Jessie Ellis-Jones (13)

TREES, TREES

Trees, trees you purify our air,
We give you the gas we cannot bear.
Trees, trees we aren't so nice,
Because we cut you with gigantic knives.
Trees, trees you are the best,
Do you wear leafy vests?
Trees, trees when you go,
We will live in sorrow.
Trees, trees you are the Earth's beloved lungs,
We like to sing you cheerful songs.
Trees, trees you are so unbelievably big,
How deep can your mighty roots dig?
Trees, trees you grew from a tiny seed,
Then after a long time you became a massive tree
Which likes to feed.

Newton Ngugi (10)

LIKE MINDS

You say you hate her because
She's always showing off,
And she says she hates you
Because you always boast
And cannot keep your mouth shut.

You say she annoys you
Because she gets better marks in tests
(But only because she cheats).
She says you annoy her
Because you think you're so much better than everyone else
(When of course you're not).

You say she looks ridiculous
Because she wears clothes that are completely out of fashion,
But she says you look ridiculous
Because you wear clothes that are in fashion
But do not suit you.

What neither of you realise,
Is that you are each other's mirror image.

Freya Carter (13)

THE DAY THE DRAGON CAME TO SCHOOL

The day the dragon came to school
The children played American pool
The teacher ran for her life
For the dragon caused such strife
More dragons came on through
Red ones, green ones, blue ones too
For school lunch we had cooked cooks
And the dragons laughed so hard they burnt the books
Now all the dragons they have gone
Yet the big bright sun still shines on.

Anne-Marie Hopkins (9)

MY PARADISE

I walk along the sandy beach,
My feet sinking in the sand.
It is so red-hot when trapped between my perfectly polished toes,
It starts to tickle.

The sand starts to look like glitter when it crumbles.
It starts to glow in my eyes.
The burning hot sun burns my clammy skin.

The deep blue sea flickers warmly.
The bright moon at night
Starts to light up the lamps along the street.
Never be afraid of what is lurking,
Lurking in the dark.

The beach is beautiful.
The beach is amazing.
So, I want to share it with you
And when I am there,
I close my eyes and pretend I'm in paradise.

Rosanna Chapman (12)

IDENTITY

People say your family are the people
that make you, you.
I disagree.
The things your family do,
that's what makes you, you.

When the people
that you love do a stupid thing,
it's you who pays the price.
My mum didn't think about what she did,
would do to me.

That's why I am against it,
suicide I mean.
It's horrible.
I'll never do it.
See, she's still teaching me
from the grave.

Samantha Davis (17)

A TYPICAL SCHOOL DAY

As I sauntered to my tutor room, I knew I was ten minutes late,
People began to stare at me, 'Better get a move on mate!'

I neared the classroom door, thinking of ways out,
But the teacher stepped in front of me,
And then began to shout.

'Do you know how many lates that's been,
That's the third one this week,
I'll have to call your parents in and have a little speak!'

'Not my parents again,' I wailed, putting on a show,
Even though I know I was walking a bit too slow.

The bell rang, telling us period one was about to start,
Next was maths and for prep I was supposed to draw a chart.

From then on the day flew by, missing prep after prep,
Now I'm hungry and I hope for lunch we get something like crepes.

The clock drew nearer to the end of the day,
'My lucky escape, thank God,' I pray.

'Chairs on the desk please,' the teacher boomed,
'Go get your bags,' I knew what loomed.

Senior tens pushing and shoving, running from locker to locker,
Passing that senior seven girl, not caring if they knock 'er.

Out of the gates, and I'm still alive,
But I have many more days, that I must survive.

Hannah Lunt (12)

DANCE

His arm, 'twas foul,
His body moved, no feeling,
An opaque beat lay peacefully,
'Twas sullen, no meaning,
Thy song played deep and mellow,
My mind at rest and dreaming,
His clothes brown and yellow,
His spirit moved on a rolling barrel,
His head lay down, to a soft growl.
''Tis thy end,' he gasped.
'No more.' He passed.

Ese-Oghene Osivwemu (13)

MUM'S CAKES

M um's cakes are the best,
U tterly better than all the rest,
M um's cakes, they taste so great,
S ometimes I eat seven or eight!

C urrant cakes, raisin or even choc chip,
A lmond, peanut or strawberry whip.
K nowing my mum will make something nice,
E ven adding some secret sugar or spice,
S o now I'll eat a cake, learn to bake!

Rhianna Watson (9)

DEVIL'S NEEDLE

Nerves racing,
Fingers tingling,
Telling me *no*
This isn't natural.
My heart trapped in my chest
Thudding against the walls,
Saying the way *out* is force.

Now I'm kept in a prison on my own
The metal walls enclosing me,
I see flat clouds and purple flowers,
Sure of their safety.
And it hits me what is to come.

Walking along,
Follow the black line,
Do not think of the building up ahead,
Just the black line,
And the cars
That's all.

Muscles stiffen
Unresponding,
Locked in fear.
Doors sweep open in front of me
And doors slid shut behind.
Sealing me in.

So many doors
All exits,
Heart telling me
Fight your way out,
Brain disagreeing,
Eyes scanning the room.
Half an hour to go.

My pupils dilating,
Legs circling each other.
On the wall
Noble beasts trapped in a frame,
Tails and manes flying,
My own loose around me, a sign of defiance.

In, early, no time to prepare
Nurse says, 'Sit down,
Hand on your hip.'

She turns away
Preparing her devil's needle.
Nerves racing,
Fingers tingling,
Telling me no
This isn't natural.

She turns back,
Needle in hand
I think of other needles,
Cleopatra's sewing, anything,
But that one.

My heart trapped in my chest
Thudding against the walls,
Saying the way *out* is force.

She steps forward,
All false smiles
Unreal, untrustable
But I do
I grip whatever's nearest,
My mother's hand
And try to relax.

'Just a small scratch,' says she,
Small
The pain exploded behind my eyes,
Coming out as a dignified whimpering
And tears.

Over.
I stumble from the hospital,
Free from the threat of the needle,
And TB,
But more the needle!

Jessica Underwood (14)

SNOW

Crisp white snow, crisp white snow
Magically falls,
Twinkles like stars
As it sprinkles like jewels.

Sparkly as glitter
It shines in the sun,
It tells you at once
That winter's begun.

Cold as the ice
It tumbles away,
Filled with Christmas spirit,
Is that nice snowy day.

Precious as treasure,
Lighter than air,
Every winter
This magic snow is there.

Heather Nixey (10)

MY JOURNEY

I was sitting on a train,
All on my own
But I had a great pain
And it was hard to ignore.

The train was letting steam,
Which I didn't like,
I thought it was mean,
But I had to let it go.

I smelt delicious food,
That I looked at very quickly,
But someone thought I was being rude,
So I quickly turned away.

My journey was nearly at its end,
And I was very glad,
I didn't like the sound of the train,
But still I was very sad!

Danielle Louise Hallowes (12)

LOVE FOREBODING

My vision, blurred by you.
A void, I'm empty without you.
Reality falls beneath my feet,
As I register your presence.
Nothing matters now.
A growing need, a pulsing fear
Rejected.
A clear pool draining of water
My life is sucked through cold, hard ground
Emptiness settles.
Lost, an abyss without reason or purpose
Reaching the edge, a waterfall cascades
Forming unknown dimensions below.
I race away with the vigorous current
Pulling me roughly through emotional turmoil
I mimic the water,
Calm from above
Teaming with disorder and frenzy below.
As I wash up on a deserted shore
Although alone, numb with cold
A hollow, harrowing hurt remains.
Muscles fight against the pain
Writhing into spasm.
Nothing will rid the phantom,
The nudge in my heart,
The shadow in my soul,
The whisper,
You.

Jasmine Ottley (17)

ABUSE ME LIKE YOU DO SO WELL

Psychopath. Crazy. Around the bend. Loopy.
That's what *you* call me. That *isn't* me.
I'm normal, aren't I?
You say weirdo. Call me mental.
Hit me, slap me, taunt me.
You hurt me, words a fist, the punch.
Calm me, soothe me, help me. No!
You hate me, loathe me, want me for dead.
So, you're crazy, loopy, around the bend.
You're a psychopath.
Yes!
Not me.
Why?
Hate me, hurt me, heal me.
Maybe!
Bully, die, abusive, cry.
Talk to me, take me, fly away and die.
Not normal, not I or you.
Bye!

Samantha Borrett (16)

IF YOU PAINT ME A COLOUR, PAINT ME . . .

If you paint me a colour, paint me yellow,
As yellow as the sun, because I am bright,
As yellow as SpongeBob, because I am always positive,
As yellow as corn, because I am sweet,
As yellow as a star, because I am shining with love.
If you paint me a colour, paint me yellow!

Jessica Barry (11)

A GAME OF GUESS WHAT IT IS

Is it a plane
Is it insane
Is it Mrs Twit
With her walking stick?
No, it's Mr Twit
Up to his old tricks
As part of 'The Twits'

But no!
It's a mole
With a nose
But it's actually some mice
With loads of woodlice
Getting eaten by cats
Who like to sleep on mats
But get eaten by foxes
Whose leader is Fantastic Mr Fox
Whose ancestors are the wolves
That need plenty of meat
So that they can live and eat
And finally they get kept as pets
And hopefully they won't go to the vets.

Navin Vithana (8)

SUMMER WAVES

Summertime is close at hand,
Roaring waves attack the sand,
Creeping up to take their prey,
Sandcastles, shells that are in their way.

At times sea bellows, at times sea cries,
At times sea jumps, at times sea dies.
When children come it backs away,
But snakes back in another day.

Laura Stevens (9)

THE FLAG THEY HAD . . .

As the sailors come in to sea,
The fear from their faces leaves to be free,
You see their wives and girlfriends pass,
Leaping and bounding the upturned mast.

Helping the wounded,
Pulling the dead,
Cleaning the wounds,
Closing with thread.

When asked what made them stay at sea,
She found an answer I can agree,
It stopped them running away from the fight,
But made them run with blood and flight.

Helping the wounded,
Pulling the dead,
Cleaning the wounds,
Closing with thread.

They said it had three colours and stripes,
As well as stars, but flying like kites,
The stronger the wind the faster it flew,
It gave us the strength, I will do too.

Helping the wounded,
Pulling the dead,
Cleaning the wounds,
Closing with thread.

A sailor asked, 'What is it to you,
You're not in my navy crew,'
But I stood up and I told him, 'No!
I have one too but mine don't glow.'

He started questioning my apparent truth,
But I'm not lying' it's not a spoof,
My flag blows high upon the mast,
In my garden it flies in cast.

Helping the wounded,
Pulling the dead,
Cleaning the wounds,
Closing with thread.

A flag to me means, trust and respect,
The sailors use it to gain and collect,
It's not the gold; it's not the gems,
But is the way the feeling stems.

Emma Howard-Felton (14)

FREEDOM

Humans have rights as you can see,
Freedom is one of them and an important one indeed,
Which is why now many suffer, fight, protest and die,
To get this special right for you and I.
For example a country called Libya,
You've heard it on the news,
It's been protesting for over three whole months,
For their freedom of never-ending dictatorship,
People are suffering from terrible deeds,
Like torturing, murdering, fighting and humiliation,
All of this to achieve a mighty goal,
The freedom for a new generation.
All of this could be done without deaths
And all these deaths could be stopped,
If one person were to step down,
His name is very well known,
His hair is rather overgrown,
And he looks like a baboon,
Can you guess who it is?
Well here's another clue to get the message through,
The person I am talking about is
A ruthless, toothless, heartless killer,
He will kill all for a luxurious villa,
And to keep power on which his heart is now set
So Libya really needs your help to make sure it won't regret,
The day it chose to forget,
And get freedom on their doorstep,
Because if freedom wasn't meant to be,
Life would change dramatically,
So what does the world need to do?
Help people get their freedom and fight back,
Hey! and you can too!
That's freedom for me and you!

Noor Sobka (12)

HE IS MY SOULMATE . . .

Handsome . . . dark . . . tall,
Compared to him I'm actually quite small.
Big muscular arms,
To hold me still and keep me calm.
Huge, dark brown eyes,
I stare into them and time just flies.
He is my soulmate . . .

Hand in hand we walk,
I enjoy nothing more but to sit and talk.
Staring eyes and soft whispers,
But we carry on as if nothing's crisper.
Side by side we stand,
Tall and proud cos he's the best in the land.
He is my soulmate . . .

Face to face we stare,
Let them watch, we don't care.
Mouth to mouth we kiss,
With him, there isn't a thing I'd want to miss
Chest to chest our hearts meet,
From the other side of the world,
I'd feel the heat.
He is my soulmate . . .

But wait!

The walls come down,
And I see your nasty frown.
I fall to the floor, reach for the door,
But all I can see is your nasty claw.
I get smaller and you get bigger,
How many more steps till he pulls the trigger?
Then it blows!

An inch from my face,
Is the knife you place.
The heat on my rib,
Is from your punch, don't fib.
The scars on my back,
Are from your good old whacks.
The crack in my heart,
Is the place where you start.
Is he my soulmate?

Priya Kaur Kohli (16)

HUSH LITTLE SISTER

Hush little sister,
Please don't cry.
I wish Mummy was here,
To sing us a lullaby.

I can see little sister,
That your arms are cut and bruised.
Don't worry because you know,
That mine were like that too.

Quickly little sister,
Run away and hide.
Daddy's coming home,
And he's drunk - no surprise.

Quiet little sister,
Please don't let him hear.
Stay under the bed for now,
Then he can't come near.

I'm sorry little sister,
That stay strong I did not.
Daddy killed me on the floor,
Whilst you were sleeping in your cot.

Oh no my little sister,
Daddy's noticed you down there!
He's getting out the belt,
And he's pulling on your hair.

Cry for help my little sister,
Don't be afraid to voice your fears.
Though the couple living next door,
May just pretend that they can't hear.

You're bleeding little sister,
And your heart is beating fast.
It's slowing little sister,
Your heart has stopped at last.

Hush now little sister,
We've given up the fight.
And at last I'll reach your hands again,
You'll sleep in my arms tonight.

Gina Hunt (11)

WHAT ARE COLOURS LIKE?

Yellow reminds me of the hot sun.
Blue reminds me of when I have fun.
White reminds me of the moon.
Silver reminds me of a spoon.
Red reminds me of firework night.
Purple reminds me of my mum hugging me tight.
Pink reminds me of sweet flowers.
Ginger reminds me of my cat who sleeps for hours.
Brown reminds me of a tree.
Black reminds me of when I can't see.
Orange reminds me of fruit.
Gold reminds me of a newt.

Mylie Freestone (7)

POLLUTION

Pollution is bad, it makes people sad.
Smoke is death, I don't like this threat.
Why do people do this?
They know that it's bad,
Just be a friendly lad.

It kills the air, it's very rare.
We breathe it in and out.
It makes me really wanna shout.
Why does this happen?

We can't see it, but we can breathe it.
Somebody kill it, so we can win it.
Somebody do it before it's too late,
It just makes me afraid.
Just be nice, or pay the price.

James Doherty-O'Brien (9)

MONEY

Money,
A make or break situation,
The world depends on it,
So something must have clicked,
Makes lives, destroys lives,
Whatever you think is,
Right?
Wrong,
Some are free with it, some are tight,
Some can manage, some lose sight,
Of the bigger picture behind all this,
As something so efficient couldn't be made by just anyone,
It takes that special someone to get it done,
It's something that can only get built upon,
Currency, Dollar, Sterling, you name it it's there,
If it's used too much the name will be stripped bare,
Some start with none,
Lots start with the perfect amount,
Or those who are spoilt have lots in their account,
But whatever happens, you just remember,
That if there was none then what would we have done without . . .
Money.

Sam Edward Thompson (14)

JUDGEMENT DAY

However bright the day
However dark the night
Where evil lurks no man shall stay
If they want to win they must fight
When the crow calls
The war must begin
When the last man falls
You know all decency has given in
The horsemen four are victorious again
Wreaking havoc and destroying order across the land
They bring malicious suffering and pain
Each one with sword in hand
They kill even though they have nothing to gain
They slaughter the innocent and butcher the poor
They will not rest until every man is slain
Be afraid when they knock at your door
Never forget there is hope
Just revive the light
Even if they slip their rope around your neck
You will need it for the final fight
Survival now depends on your might
Do not fear, you will not perish
You must fight
Think of the ones you cherish
Hope and salvation shall be your sword and shield
And with them you shall strike at their single black heart
They will not yield
You must fight one last time before you depart
And now the time has come when we must part.

Rhys Barnwell (12)

CHEW ON THIS THOUGHT

This was a world,
a world that I knew,
and it's thanks to you
that it's gone.
I'm telling you this!
It won't go amiss.
Can't you see
that it's wrong.
The lions, the tigers,
the small chimpanzees,
the jaguars and
the bumblebees.
Deforestation,
habitats gone.
One thousand then twenty
and now only one.
Brought to their deaths
by Man.
Sold for money, medicine
and rugs.
Voodoo rituals,
illegal drugs.
This has to stop!
I'm telling you now.
They think they don't know any better.
So I'm stating this right here
for you.
Spelling it letter by letter.
Hunting is wrong!
Poaching and traps.
Knives, guns and poisons.
The animals you see
are saying this through me.
For when they are gone so are we.
So chew on this thought
because I know it's a good one
and think what you do
that is wrong.

No more miaows
or delicate tweeting
for when they are gone
they are gone.

Rachel Stephenson (12)

FLASHBACK

Crouching in the shadows
With wide and fearful eyes,
Listening to the turmoil and constant crying,
A young girl waits, helpless and alone.

She slips through silently to her house,
Jarring her feet on the rubble around.
Through a crack in the shell of her house
She stares with sorrow at the devastation beyond.

The deafening drumming of gunfire fills the air,
Throwing up flurries of dust in its wake.
Screaming and yelling surrounds her,
Like she is trapped in a cavern of destruction.

Another shot. In the distance another man falls.
Crash! Another house falls under its own weight.
Her Afghan home town, now a jumble of rubble -
All that is left of her childhood.

She starts to run, blindly, blundering,
Not noticing the rubble that cruelly spikes her feet.
A bullet whooshes by just an inch from her head.
In fright, she scampers into an abandoned house for cover.

'Where are you?' she whispers, panting,
Tears of dread and loneliness filling her eyes.
She has nothing, nothing, only the vain hope
That one day her beloved family will return to her.

Rebekah Baugh (14)

MY HERO

Where's Daddy?
The last time I saw him was when he went off to war,
I remember how he looked at me
I want him back.

Where's Daddy?
He's gone to fight the bad people.
He told me to be brave and not to cry.
I want him back.

Where's Daddy?
My daddy went to fight for the country,
I don't know when my daddy is coming home.
I want him back.

Where's Daddy?
Daddy has gone off on an adventure,
When will I see my daddy again?
I want him back.

Where's Daddy?
I saw my mummy crying,
I looked into her eyes, now I know
My daddy is not coming home.

Daddy is here, I can see him.
Every time I close my eyes, I can see him.
I can feel his presence surrounding me.
Now I know where Daddy is, he is right here with me.

Bethany Dillon (14)

HE'S GONE

I look for him,
I search, search for the glimpse of his copper hair,
For his deep blue eyes
Mirroring the ocean perfectly.

I suck in a deep sharp breath,
The air scrapes down my throat and tangles itself on my tonsils,
I feel as if I have been stabbed, stabbed straight into my heart.
I can see him now . . .

I snap my eyes shut, the image is unbearable,
However, I can still see his face, the face of others surrounding him,
The horror, the fear, the desperation, the knowing.
A single tear trickles and crawls its way down my face.

My eyes are open now - wide open my gaze has shifted to another man,
His face, his face, if only there were words to describe how he looked
Without another second passing he leapt, dived
Into the jaws of death awaiting him.

A fallen angel in the midst of this hellish scene
A peace looked to have swept over him,
His body delicately fluttering through the air
Suddenly, his body slapped the surface of the ocean,
I grabbed, snatched for a hand that wasn't there.

It's nearly over now, if the hand of horror will ever let me go
We are floating away,
The few of us selfishly saved
Why me? I am nothing special, I don't want to go, to leave him. Not me.

The last of the flares have been let off,
The last prayers of the people stranded,
The last glimmer of hope is fading away
Into burnt out embers to be taken away with the wind.

One last pitiful groan from her and the unsinkable ship has taken her last breath.

Abi Slater (14)

LADIES MAN

Whenever I was down you'd always pick me up,
Whenever I needed a shoulder to cry on you'd always appear!
You were always a moral person,
Who made the room as bright as the sun,
You only ever had one side and that was good,
You never said a bad word about anybody
And no one had anything bad to say about you.

You would always try and convince me and Mum to hop on the back,
'Come on, quick, we'll be back in 3.5!'
Top to toe in leather, helmet in your hand,
Squeak, squeak as you'd enter the room,
You'd zoom past nearly blowing me over, trying to impress the ladies!
Whenever anybody needed something doing
All we would hear is, 'Leave it with me.'

You may have left our sight but never our minds,
You'll always look over us like an angel,
You will always have happy memories, no bad,
We will stay happy as you'd want us to and remember you forever.
Rest in peace Uncle Jai. Good night.

Ashna Avda (14)

FUTURE

Do you ever think of the men that perished on the battlefield?
They lost their life for us.

Do you ever think of their families?
They shed tears for us.

Do you ever think of the men in Afghanistan?
They fight for us.

Do you ever think of the agony and suffering they see?
They watch for us.

Will you ever think of these individuals?
I know I will, because in the end, it's all been for us and our future.

Libby Howitt (13)

THE BOY IN STRIPED PYJAMAS

We sit here day after day
Hoping something good will come our way
Why am I here?

I want to be free and run around
But when I'm here I can't make a sound
Why am I here?

I feel trapped without any space
Hopefully one day I'll get out of this cold place
Why am I here?

I'm getting thinner and I'm starving
In remembrance I started wall carving
Why am I here?

We all wear a striped uniform
Awaiting the oncoming storm
Why am I here?

I'm just a child, only fourteen
I don't deserve this kind of dream
Why am I here?

The soldiers run around
Making sure we don't make any noisy sound
Why am I here?

I feel in prison without any room
I feel the darkness surround me in a gloom
Why am I here?

We children smell burning
Just thinking about it is stomach churning
Why am I here?

I feel like an animal stuck in an enclosure
I'll get out of here I know I will, I'm sure
Why am I here?

It's so confusing why I'm here
But is it simply because I'm a Jew?

I don't belong here
Let me out of this prison cell
One day I'll be free, free to be who I want to be
Someday I'll feel like I belong in this world.

Megan Thompson (14)

ONE STEP

They take a deep breath,
They'll do it together,
Hand in hand forever,
I'd do anything to see them again.

One step to change their life,
To change our life, to change my life,
One step, one step is all it took,
I'd do anything to see them again.

Floating. Soaring. Gliding,
With that one step they left,
They left a burning flame, and fell into a sea of blue,
I'd do anything to see them again.

Looking out onto the city they loved,
Onto everything they'd ever wanted,
They knew, it wasn't supposed to end this way, not now,
I'd do anything to see them again.

Plunging deeper and deeper into the sea of blue,
They know now, they know it's the end,
The pain will be gone soon,
I'd do anything to see them again.

No longer are they flying,
Instead they are at peace. Resting, sleeping, lying,
Mum and Dad united in Heaven. Together forever,
I'd do anything to see them again.

Francesca Saberton (14)

MY CHILDHOOD

How can I forget?
The pain that's engraved on my mind,
The pain I can still feel.

Was it my fault?
He only did it because of me,
Did I make this happen?

Could I have stopped it?
If only I'd told someone, I could have stopped it,
Why didn't I help her?

How can I stop the memories?
Have you ever woken up, scared after a nightmare?
I have, but mine was the memories of my childhood,
The pain I can still feel.

What happens when you feel you have failed someone?
You start blaming yourself,
Wondering if you could, have stopped it.

As a child your parents don't expect you to look after them,
But if your mum or dad needed help,
You would help them.

What if?
What if it was your dad causing all the pain?
My childhood was taken away from me,
I watched my dad tear our family apart strip by strip.

Now I know it wasn't my fault,
I wasn't to blame,
I couldn't have stopped it,
I didn't fail anyone.

When you are nine years old
And being abused by your father,
How could you have helped your helpless mother,
From the claws of her abusive husband?

Hollie King (13)

THE RIGHT PATH

Should I leave, should I stay?
Be a brave, courageous idol
Following the same path my brother did,
Or be a frightful man full of concern.

I know, if I choose to leave
The fear will fill the air once again,
But what should I do?
My dream is to be a national hero.

My instincts tell me it's the right decision,
But my conscience is overpowered by fright,
It feels as if I'm lost in the woods
Not knowing what is the right path to follow.

I feel like a coward if I don't go,
But at the same time I realise the jeopardy,
The thought of my parents losing another son,
Would feel like mass destruction to them.

My heart is in throbbing pain,
I need to go,
I have made my decision,
Sorry Mum and Dad, but my country needs me!

Nicola Wan (14)

CAMELS ARE LUMPY

Camels are hairy and I find them scary.
Camels are bumpy and lumpy
Just like pyramids; humpy.

They live in Egypt where it is sandy and sunny,
Near all the pharaohs and the mummies.

Ben Wood (8)

SUICIDE ALONE

The children and I stand at the door,
Watching husband and Daddy going off to the war.
How will I cope now he has gone?
Just me and the children on our own.

'I'll be back soon,' he says as we wave goodbye
As I hear these words I start to cry.
All we can do now is wait
And pray that God will keep him safe.

'I'll be back soon,' he says
And every day I have been waiting, waiting.
Years gone by,
And still all I am doing is waiting, waiting.

'I'll be back soon,' my sons say as they go to the war,
I have never felt so alone before.
I am all alone,
All alone, and still I am waiting, waiting.

The telegraphs came one by one,
Husband and sons dead and gone.
I put a bullet through my brain,
No one to wait for every again.

No more waiting,
No more worrying,
United in Heaven,
Happy again.

Sheryl Lai (14)

STORY OF THE RESISTANCE

Are there minutes or seconds left before this hideous execution?
This cold-blooded murder,
This walk of fate.
We sold our souls and failure isn't an option.

The distant roar hits me; the sound of hunger - for justice, for blood,
Well-armed soldiers laughing, just laughing.
Mocking the pointlessness of human existence,
But appearances are deceptive.

I forge ahead into the pathetic herd of lemmings,
Eyes wide with fright with my brothers by my side.
I pass my friend, a decaying corpse swelling with mindless maggots,
The cloth above us strangely motionless in the wind.

The next pause is deadly, truly deadly. So many men, so many options,
The faces of nervously rushing people flooding around me, trying to get away.
Trying to get away from the finger-like wisps,
But there is no escape. There is no way out.

A pang of sadness hits me; with every breath I heave,
We have to fight for every freedom we have.
Nothing is certain but death,
But old soldiers never die, they simply fade away.

Emily Ansell (13)

I REMAIN

In high winds or gusty shores,
It maybe safe in pores,
Safe in fine net,
But my pathwalk will always
Remain gathered,
Whether in spite or doubt.

Tino Karase (13)

A VICTIM'S CRY

I was hurt, unloved and afraid,
Unable to speak or cry.
Scared I would not be saved,
As mocking words were heavyweights, preventing me to fly.

Cruel jibes I faced in the morning,
And sneers without love or hope.
Photos of me happier were haunting,
As then my own reflection, confirmed something that suddenly broke.

Drowning in my own shadow,
I couldn't feel my voice.
Screaming out from my misty bedroom window,
I knew I had to make a choice!

'Stand up,' whispered my confidence,
A weak sound I hadn't recently heard.
But hurtful memories cornered me with an iron fence,
So still, I remained a quiet, caged bird.

In the morning, I realised I should take it no longer,
Never look at myself again with weakness or doubt.
Those jibes and mocks had made me stronger,
But now at my bully, I will shout.

'There was no mercy in your pointing finger,
Or in those piercing eyes that stared at me.
Remember my friend, with all your pride still lingered,
One finger that pointed my way, back at you, there was three.

Don't you remember your long speeches?
That droned on about how great you are.
But now, Holy ears hear nothing but un-Godly screeches,
And tut in disapproval, as they know Heaven and you is far.

For my sisters, you were wrong.
For it was never about what you knew was right,
Life is more than your proud song.
Look past your nose, for Heaven is beyond your sight.

And out of your grasp without my pardon,
Out of sight without my say.
But while your abuse continued, my heart did not harden;
Of course I will forgive you, but only if you pray.

Pray to God about yourself,
And for Him to forgive you fully.
For I will forget you, and put your memory at the back of my shelf,
But feel happy, you will no longer be a bully.'

Rachel Senior (14)

GOODBYE

My friend is moving from this place,
I wish I could fit inside her suitcase,
She comes from another country you see,
One that is far away from me.
I know that she cannot stay,
She eventually had to move away.

At times I cry myself to sleep at night,
Thinking of the day that she takes flight,
Across the sea,
Away from me.
I know that she cannot stay,
She eventually had to move away.

She is my best friend you see,
We are like sisters, her and me,
We have been through so much together,
I will remember her forever.
I know that she could not stay,
She eventually had to move away.

Megan Watson (14)

THE FRUIT BAT

Sucking gleefully on a sugary peach,
Every night below the celestial body of stars,
Creamy apricots, plums and berries,
In a dream floating to the ring of Mars,
Feeding chiefly on nectar or succulent fruit,
Its paper thin wings and wreathing around the fur,
Still dreaming of slushy avocadoes,
Just above the bed of watercress but does it matter?
Glancing with its fiery eyes waiting for dusk,
For the squishy squashy mango, or for the slurps of figs,
When the ivory cheesy moon converts into a tusk!

Kishara Puvanendiran (10)

GOODBYE LULLABY

The morning brings a new light,
that covers me,
echoes fill the room,
whispering words of hope and dreams,
that weren't meant for me.

I sit alone in an empty room,
and I hear a choir of violins
break through the silence,
haunting this dark place,
when crying their bittersweet harmony.

Thunder shakes the ground,
all I hear is the beat of my heart,
shattered again and again,
holding onto nothing,
but it still breathes a life of its own.

My fingers move over the keys,
reaching for the words that can't be spoken,
this piano's broken song,
bring back simpler times,
when everything was what it seemed.

As this day turns to dusk,
let the crescendo turn to stars,
but before I close my eyes,
I want to thank the music,
for being by my side.

And so I pray my friend,
that as my days draw to an end,
you will write a last song for me,
one sorrowful note that lives for eternity,
I ask, will there be a goodbye lullaby for me?

Abigail Foster (14)

A BRIEF HISTORY OF FERRY MEADOWS

What does the school boy see
As he flies his kite or climbs a tree
At Ferry Meadows?
    A country park
    To walk with pleasure
    To sail or cycle
    A place for leisure.
What did the Saxon farmer see
As he harvested land that would one day be
Ferry Meadows?
    Fields to plough
    Crops to eat
    Fertile land
    Water sweet.
What did the Roman soldier see
From his fort on the land that would one day be
Ferry Meadows?
    A training ground
    Far from Rome
    To drill and march
    And dream of home.
What did the woolly mammoth see
As he stomped the land that would one day be
Ferry Meadows?
    Ice, ice baby . . .

Jordan Grinyer (12)

MY LITTLE ROBIN

He floats through the air
But I see no wing or hair,
Could it be Grandad?

Could he be a dove?
A symbol of undying love,
Is that you Grandad?

Are you a sparrow?
But no you are a robin,
My little robin.

With a dark red breast,
Beautiful dark brown wings,
And deep hazel eyes.

You came to us then
Dad said you had returned
As my little bird.

Imogen Pope (14)

THE LIFE OF THE PAST

I am the dinosaur,
I am in the prehistoric life,
Dinosaurs move around as if they are going to attack,
Some of them fly in the blue, vast sky,
When they are dead you can observe the rotten fossils scattered everywhere,
Proterceratops, the extra tiny one
Moves swiftly and soundly on the Planet Earth,
Colossal dinosaurs stomping on the ground,
Boom, boom! they go,
Flying dinosaurs zoom,
Sea dinosaurs go, *splish, splosh, splish, splosh!*
Dinosaurs sometimes kill triceratops, but beware,
Without them knowing!

Prutthikan Puvanendiran (8)

SILENT SHOUT

I shout, but it is as quiet and serene as a deserted island.
No one seems to notice me.
Am I invincible?

I scream in an empty room, but even I myself can't seem to hear
my own echoes. How unrealistic can this be?
Am I a statue?

I roar like a wounded, angry lion,
but my voice sounds like that of a peaceful lullaby,
putting a child to its sleep.
Am I a shadow?

The image in my mirror is heard more than myself.
How can this silence be so over-powering?
Am I a slave?

My tears roll down my face in silence,
making a sound known to them only, trying to give a sign,
like a roaring, roaring thunder.

Am in danger? Where can I run to? Who will hear
my cry for help? Everything seems like whispers. Silence
has taken over.

Could this be my silent shout? This is my
silent shout. Hoping tomorrow will bring happiness
to my shuttered words.

Theresa Mwewa (15)

MUSIC

Black notes on a white page
Contrasting cultures united in a sound
We forget about discrimination and come out of our set cage
We put aside our differences as this shared passion is found

The strength of a pulse is magical really
We can relate to it as it expresses our feelings
Normally we are trying to please others
But for a minute we can roam freely
And we forget about what others think as our voices hit the ceiling

Music is one of a kind
I can honestly say there is nothing like it
It contains the power to turn hate blind
And such a gift shouldn't be recognised as noise, but as art.

Eleanor Sutton (14)

THE WINNER STILL LOSES

The thing about wars is that the winner still loses,
And how many he loses the loser chooses.
Sure a picture can say a thousand words,
And an action a thousand more,
But how many does a bullet say?
So many people, who could tell, are not alive today.

The thing about wars is their pretence at high glamour.
To be a hero and fight for their country, the people clamour.
The bayonets glint like sun-played diamonds,
Wisps of gas woven into nymphs dance among the charging soldiers,
And the bursting of a mine strikes a perfect beat.
Too bad it bursts beneath a soldier's feet.

The thing about the war was that it was fear-riddled.
The men waited with the rats, rain-drenched and mud-clothed.
The seconds ticking down to go over the top was maddening,
Under cannon and machine fire they all fell,
And their torn away souls prayed God knew they meant well.

Niall Caplis (15)

I DISAGREE

No one notices the silent child
Waiting every day for his mother to come
But as he remains by the door
He gets the same, a father who makes him run
As the belt is received and the hand is raised
The boy doesn't recoil, but in fact sits still
Wincing at every hit and sobbing silently
Reluctantly obeying his father's will

The boy doesn't laugh or play as he should
Instead he hides behind a closed door
Praying his father doesn't find him
As his glass-like body can take no more
The boy's first kiss, the father will never know
A ball game they shall never share
A scabby knee and a plaster needed
But the father doesn't care

The father should have guilt to remind him
But this guilt he does not feel
The boy has the bruises and the scars
To remind him that his past is real
Children learn to smile from their parents
But what is a smile when it is fake?
No alterations, no turning back
For this is the only road the boy can take

He has no choice
He is unfree
The boy cannot be saved
But I disagree.

Gursharan Kaur Dhanda (15)

MY DOG TOBY

I have a dog called Toby
who is a little rascal!
Although he is small
and not very tall,
he thinks he can fly
and touch the sky.
He chews my flower pots
but I still love him lots.
Once I woke up and this is what I heard,
Toby barking at a bird.
He does not bite,
only when we play fight.
He cuddles up to me at the end of the day,
I love him more than words can say!

Emma Coxon (12)

JUST MY BIKE

Misty is the mare grazing by the gate.
She has the speed of six stallions,
Her ebony mane and tail contrast against her shiny coat.
With a turn of her midnight reins she changed direction
But always with a twinkle of her eye.

With my glossy black riding hat I race down the track,
My hair quivering in the wind.
Misty's pelt suddenly shimmers,
As the sunlight reflects off it.
She rears up.
I lose control, but cling onto her reins.
I steer her back home,
I de-mount her,
I take a last glimpse back at her,
She's not my horse anymore,
She's only just . . . my bike.

Emma Caro (10)

UNDER THE SEA

When I'm under the sea,
It's my favourite place to be.
Don't look in the dark,
Because you might see a shark.
Stingrays you will see,
Swimming alongside me.

Seaweed is so green,
Octopus is so mean.
They spray some ink,
You'll start to sink.
Watch the turtles swim,
As they dive out then in.

I've run out of air,
It seems so unfair.
I'm up at the surface,
Now at the base.
I wonder when,
I can go diving again.

Jasmine Shuard (12)

MELODY

Melody flowing through my ears,
into my heart and there it stays.
Brushing over the heavy ivory keys;
Wondering whether changing key would suit best.
But no, the lullaby is suited
to all of my needs.

Freya Jones (16)

I STARE AT MY REFLECTION

I stare at my reflection in the mirror
But all I see . . .
Is a dull face staring back at me
No emotion nor smile
Just a single teardrop

But as I look within
I realise the time bomb within me
Ready to explode into countless shivers . . .
And it is then when I realise just how easy it is . . .

To hold everything inside of you
Having no trust in nobody nor yourself
A waiting room . . .
Emotional pain that is reaching its very limit
Ready to break through the wall
It is then when you realise how hard it is to put these broken shivers back where they belong
Where a soul once existed
But got caught up in a hurricane that set it free into the empty space
So . . .

You're left with a broken soul
That can only be faked by a smile
A smile that you bought just to say that you're okay
A label so common it's on every corner you turn to . . .

But can happiness be bought?
Maybe not. Maybe yes
But only in all eyes, but your own
It's a beautiful disaster that you may never forget . . .
But hey! Who am I to say? I no longer own a soul, argh!

Kristina Radzeviciute (16)

THE WALK OF SHAME

Sunflower yellow stilettos walking down the road of shame
The dress more dirty this morning than it was the night before.
The succulent flesh cooked to perfection
Dripping with condensation from waiting to be eating
Will you stuff it?
The morning ice cold shoulder of vodka in the jacket pocket.
A cup from the deli and a lukewarm 150ml bottle of Coke.
Condensation dripping down the vodka.
Sitting under a bridge at 6am
The village hobos just sitting there staring at you
Pouring a bottle of silver into your cup.
Mouths dripping with saliva.
Never sleeps.
Their motorbikes.
In a limo on the sunroof singing to my tune.
Can't stand being lonely.
I'm in your blood.
Tell your mother
It's hurricane season.
I see you there in my eye fluid.

Nicole Kinsella (16)

SUMMER

Summer is here
Summer is here
Hear the sizzling sausages on the barbecue outside
Feel the scorching sun tanning your skin
Summer is here
Hear the children splashing in the mini paddling pools
Feel the joy buzzing around in a furious energy
Summer is here
Teenagers digging out their bathing suits
Because summer is finally here!

Worthwhile Breeze Nkomo (14)

DANCING IN THE HEAT

Sit in sweat and gaze, and waste the time away;
Pretending we don't see them, lick our lips and sway.
All knowing at least one of them is almost too far gone,
But glistening necks and glittered cans with empty hearts roll on.

Quaking heels and nails scrape the floor in heat.
Dripping endlessly like stripped and bludgeoned meat -
Bodies curved and finished, sigh in octaves ancient,
Whilst hungry, waiting monsters breed silent abasement.

Slipping thighs and quiet minds, interchanging thoughts,
Growing airs of madness in our weakening cohorts.
Every colour darkens round the muted, dim fatigue,
Each flavour once a blossom, feeds dangerous intrigue.

They may become one's habit on warm as brandy nights
And falling, chalky skies watch from soiled purple heights.
Slow and haughty lunacy in grey, gargled addiction,
Bitten lips and tampered skin - *'love'* in frank infliction.

Even in the thickening of hot and heavy breath,
Spit in throats of children, clotting air attempting rest.
Trickling dusty liquors seep into the trance
Of the wild, sudoral keepers, that come to watch us dance.

Gabriella Forson (17)

WE ARE ALL LAMP POSTS

A lamp post sees only a small circle of the world.
Some light upon a mere few feet of street,
Others a vast stretch of highway
But a tiny piece of universe nonetheless.
Occasionally you find that the pool of yellow cast by one
Overlaps with that of another,
But not often - they are solitary creatures.
Now and then something passes through the space
Created and inhabited by an onlooking lantern
And changes its life forever.
We are all lamp posts.

Sarah Collingham (16)

MY SISTER

You never comprehend the vast part,
Your little sister takes in your touched heart,
She is profoundly funny and has generally the most money,
Among our family of four.
She doesn't drain her own,
In our family as a miser she is renown.
Our relationship is the most near.
And when we have a fight we have no fear,
That this feud will never end.
She's my true friend.
She is always there for me,
So as you see,
We have got each other's backs.
There is no quality in her that lacks.
We always fight.
But we well as might,
Just get along.
She will be my true friend,
Till the end.

Sara Ahmad (11)

WORDS

Words can't describe what you mean to me
Words can't describe you or me
Words can't describe how you make me feel
Words are just words
Feelings are just feelings
I just wanted to say I love you
They are words with feelings
Words that describe how I feel about you.

Nicole Richardson (14)

PROM

The bell rings, it's the end of class
Everyone running to get home
Groups of girls pass and pass
And I stand alone.

I'm going to the prom by myself
Just to make my mother happy
Do my make-up and look at the mirror on the shelf
And I stand alone.

I'm the geek
No one likes and doesn't want to be friends with
At break they shout pathetic freak
And I stand alone.

Expensive dress and gorgeous heels
Climbing off the 66 bus I stand well clear
Girls and boys turn up in hot wheels
And I stand alone.

People chatting, cheering, dancing
Music blaring, decorations galore
People kissing, laughing, prancing
And I stand alone.

Last dance is the slow dance
Couples holding each other and loving each other
I'm never ever going to get a chance
And I stand alone.

I think to myself when I'm walking home
Along the canal side, under the lampposts
I'm practically invisible, not even chrome
And I jump . . . alone.

Jade Louise Piggott (17)

BRAND NEW DAY!

Sitting in my bedroom, staring out to space
Wondering what's wrong with a human race.
Who is gonna get me, who's friend or foe?
I just don't wanna live like this anymore.

Thoughts black as raven entering my mind
Cord looks inviting hanging from the blind.
This is like crazy! I rummage through my shelf,
Grab a pen and write a letter to myself.

'Tell me where you're going - I will show you, how
If you wanna change your life - live your future right now!
Life is like a circus - Cirque du Soleil:
Giddy up, giddy up - it's a brand new day!

If you lost your way make a new one right here.
Hack it through the jungle and your path will clear.
Open up your mind - tell me what you see
Don't cry, don't lie, don't try - just be!

Tell me what you're missing and look inside
Everything you wanted - you can find.
Things that you are capable will blow your mind!
Your heartbeat strong and your future's bright!

The descendants of Genghis - we are mighty strong.
Like the Devil's apprentice - it's a little bit wrong.
Like footprints in history - it's a bit of a mystery.
We are survivors from the day we're born.

Open up your mind - tell me what you see.
What you plan today, tomorrow will be
Tomorrow will be.
Tomorrow . . . tomorrow . . . tomorrow . . .

Life's a roller coaster and a bumpy ride.
Haters and the infidels can take a hike;
Bully boys and ignorants can't ruin my chance!
'Cause I'm shaping my dream with my both two hands!

Life is like a poem - so make it rhyme.
Weave it to the beat and make it shine.
Feel it in your soul and take your time.
Giddy up, giddy up - 'cause you will be fine!

Future's like a dragon so ride it like a sea.
Nobody's bothering my life and me!
Busy up your mind like the streets of Bombay.
Giddy up, giddy up - it's a brand new day!

Zack Homeless (11)

LYING GLASS

He turns me around
holds my shoulders firmly
fingers wrapped
around collarbone
and forces me to look
into the reflected world
guides me, as if more
familiar with each angle
than myself;

His hands loosen,
white prints left on
papery skin,
then move across
each sweeping bone
a rack either side
of the essence of life, love
that which swells, shrinks
to an unstable time frame
an interrupted rhythm which
often pumps too fast, slow,
tired of existing
at the core of the body.

He says, 'Look,
each length of precious ivory
stretches like an archer's bow.'
I look away, ashamed of my flesh;
I do not see what he sees.

My eyes study his head
which fits neatly in the curve
from my shoulder to neck
as he notices the disgust
illustrated by subtle stains
across each cheekbone
which reveal the hate
I fail to conceal.
The coated skull turns,
an order gently floats
from him to me,
mouth to ear,
whispering, 'Close your eyes.'
I trust him, thankful that I can
erase the gross outline which

stares, as if made from cold glass itself,
at its clone;
the clone which I seem
unable to wash away
with water or ipecac or
my diminishing willpower.

His hand runs down my spine
as if faintly painting my body
in two, the shallow thump
echoes an ostinato
composed by each vertebra
that is raised against pale skin.
This scaffolding shows desperation
to free itself from the
suffocating flesh,
to break through
the soft shell and shine
sharp and superior,
an ivory carving,
precious and perfect.

He cups his hands,
one around each hip bone
and manages almost to form a fist
against my skin
which is stretched taut
like a canvas framed by bone.

'If I pull hard enough,' he utters,
'I can split you open.'
I do not doubt his strength.
'I can snap your toothpick skeleton
like I would a twig.'
I take this as a compliment,
try to hide my pride.

Emma Boyns (17)

THE END OF THE YEAR

September
The warm of the summer still hangs in the air,
A gentle breeze is tossing my hair.
I walk alone,
I walk in a daze.
You left me alone in a warm summer haze.

October
The next month arrives and the time passes by,
Shrivelling leaves tossing out of the sky,
All other people
Seem distant from me,
As I sit without you beneath the ash tree.

November
The cold of the winter soon starts to arrive,
The birds are migrating, barely alive.
It all doesn't matter,
You're no longer there.
And now that you're gone I just can't seem to care.

December
Christmas has come but I don't send a card.
The ground is so brittle, the ice is so hard.
The snow doesn't fall.
The world's stiff with frost.
As cold as my heart for the love that I lost.

January
Festive decorations start to disappear.
My face feels like stone and I don't shed a tear.
Nobody can see
That I'm tortured inside.
They can't know how it haunts me to know that you've died.

February
The 14th of February: Valentine's Day,
My love stays in tatters, my heart in decay.
I look at the cards
That I'll never send,
And I know more than ever that all love must end.

March
Spring has arrived and the winter is gone.
Every day of my life becomes one day too long.
I stay solitary,
And my clothes remain black.
I grieve for the person I'll never get back.

April
There's new birth, new life, and new things all around,
And the song of the birds is a beautiful sound.
But the joy has all vanished,
It's no longer there.
Because nothing can mend where my heart has a tear.

May
The showers and sunshine all come in May,
And on the outside there is nothing to say,
But inside I scream,
And inside I cry.
My only wish now is to join you and die.

June
The summer brings suffering, mourning and pain,
And sometimes I think that I'm going insane.
I know that you're dead.
I know that you've gone.
But my heart is still telling me that I am wrong.

July
The strawberries ripen, the sun's beating down,
But I cannot make myself smile or frown.
Outside it's hot,
But inside me it's cold.
I no longer care how events will unfold.

August
The last month of summer, a year has passed by,
I make my decision, decision, to die.
The edge of the cliff,
Looks over the sea.
I step off the edge, and I set my soul free.

Anna Kelly (12)

DANCING BEAR

He leaps,
He shakes,
He hops,
He quakes.

They cheer,
They laugh,
They clap,
As they whip him.

Do they know how he feels?
They most likely don't even care!
For what is he to them?
Only a dancing bear!

Eleanor Smith (11)

BOURNEMOUTH

Let me introduce you to my special place:
Somewhere I can relax and have fun.
Where I can smell the fresh fish and chips cooking.
Where I can get covered in the golden sand.
Somewhere I can hear the swishing of the sea.
This place is special to me because I love it.
This place is called Bournemouth!

Olivia Faye Mcewan (12)

I SEE YOU

I see you, do you see me?
It's strange, mysterious, how can it be?
I see you everywhere I go,
But no one else seems to know.
When I'm asleep and tucked up tight,
When Big Ben rings and strikes midnight,
I see you when I am dreaming,
The next morning, I wake up screaming.
I see you on my doorway stair,
I see you floating in the air.
Do you exist? Reveal yourself!
And please stop sitting on my shelf!

Katy Hopson (12)

THE CREATURE

It crept along the passage,
this dark, vicious
and mysterious creature.

It was stalking its prey
a mysterious and
beautiful spectacle.

It was of course:
a cat.

Billie Powell (12)

THE SPELL OF THE SEASONS

The spring comes forth in all its glory
It shouts, 'Let the spring begin its story.'
The carpet finally turns around
The greenery is finally found
Everything yellow, blue and green
Are the only things that are actually seen
There should be a carpet that is visible
But to mortals the carpet is invisible
That should make them miserable
For they only see the flowers beside
But mortals' minds do not decide
That spring's palace is to hide
Right there at the end of the long, long, long, long carpet
Where nature all first met.

The summer strides forward to claim its throne
Finally summer is no longer alone
A shade of yellow and a hue of green
On his attire is now seen
These are the colours at his easel by the way
No more colours sit at his easel today
He doesn't need more anyway
He fills his easel with dots and bobs
Lines, squiggles, stripes and knobs
But suddenly his easel vanishes,
He looks up and who steps in, than . . .

Autumn, his evil face and flickering smile
Beady eyes, yellow and vile
Show no mercy for trees. 'Abracadrabra,' he'll say
All the trees will begin to sway
The leaves will fall to the ground
And Autumn likes it colourful around
So he'll turn them red, green, brown, purple, yellow
And orange until who arrives but . . .

Winter, he's in a bad mood
He's had to clean up Autumn's mess
When he was about to eat some food
He takes his fury out on the land
First storm from the east with their blusters begins
It really is quite grand

Then Winter will get out his snow gun and snow will fall
The amount is not small
Winter hasn't just begun
Winter has won!

Ifeatu Ikechukwu Obiora (10)

COLOUR ME CHIRAL

Mirror, mirror on the wall -
Who's the queen and who's the fool?
You feed me this chiasmus through
Your chiral, chiral glass
So the honey tones are
Viscous blue,
Oh! What I thought I was,
Would, should, might ever be;
Swallowed in your laterals.
Two eyes brown,
Two eyes burn,
Three lips smile and
One head turns
Towards the side where nothing lies
But nine lives churning burnout words:

One is gold with broken wings,
One laughs
One runs circles -
Crying saline rings.
Three others sit in marked remorse
Drenched in sanguine,
Loved and lost.
The spinning trio dance untouched
Behind a line I cannot cross.

The scarlet ribbons wave behind the
Immaculate deceit,
Dull distance presses from all sides
And hissing whispers, whispers,

Born separative, born broken?
I,
I need only one loose shard,
But my selfish self demands
I must own every single part.

Mirror, mirror on the floor -
Who's not breathing anymore?

Polly Fullerton (17)

THE PAGE

Empty desolate, deserted:
A hostile land of the possible and impossible;
Abandoned by Time's ghost millenniums ago,

Submerged by a deep pool of echoing silence,
Disturbed only by a drop of ink . . .

Ripples of life engulfing the dead world.
Scribbles of blackness channelling meaning into the blank earth,
Formless figures evolving from mere imagination.

Time reversing and elapsing,
A future weaving with an intricate pattern,
By the mind of a master; a creator.

The words that inhabit and nurture this new earth;
Some kind, some harsh, some an unsolvable enigma.

Abruptly, words lunge out of their flat, papery lair,
Black and vicious, striking with violent blows,
Frantic, only caring to gouge comfort from my mind,
To feed on and absorb my soul.

I shield against their ferocious onslaught,
Distraught, but eventually surrendering.

But then another -
A word of tranquil serenity,
Silhouetted, a furtive glimmer of Hope's trueness.

Moving lightning quick to intercept,
The tendrils of light that slip elusively to bind their darkness,
The words of darkness at Death's command,
Obliterated by kindness, hope and love.

Simple black scribbles woven into a page,
Or a life, in a world.

Sarah Ladd (13)

RUMMY

The sweetest sound of nature echoes clear,
Above the heads of everybody here,
As spirits tumble, tremble, dive and roll,
The bodies red as ginger, black as coal,
Tensions rising with the saffron sun,
Cursing whispers heard from everyone,
Placid hope rests in tormented minds,
All are keen not to be left behind.

One horse, as bay as conkers can be shown,
Blinks and watches, knows what can't be known.
He fully knows how fast that he can move,
His staying power's what he's got to prove.
Round and round and up and down they go,
The emerald grass in breeze begins to blow,
'When will they start?' words flutter like a moth,
The immortal tape is rising, and . . . they're off!

One, two, three, four, as they set off, hooves pound,
Tearing up the sacred Aintree ground,
The fences, taller, rise in majesty,
Will they bring victory or travesty?
But as they take the whole thing in their stride,
Eating up the turf, all side by side,
One creature inches out from all the rest,
Dark all over, with a snow-white crest.

He stays ahead, an engine finely made,
His victory, it seems, cannot be swayed,
But conker-horse, Red Rum is his real name,
Who throws himself into this jumping game,
Has not yet fallen; this is the crowd's song:
'Red Rum has not yet put a fetlock wrong!'
And as to final fences they do race,
Rummy is still king, but Crisp the ace.

The final fence has now been cleared at last,
But the excitement of the crowd's not passed,
As Crisp still thuds along the chopped-up track,
The public think there's now no turning back,
'He'll win,' they say, 'and he deserves it too.'
When all at once, and straight out of the blue,
Another horse comes flying out of the haze
Of turf and branch, his mane and hooves ablaze.

For Rummy won't believe that all is lost,
He'll carry on, no matter what the cost,
He feels the message bore into his brain,
The jockey tells him o'er and o'er again,
'Go on! Go on!' he screams, though with no sound,
He knows the horse is slowly gaining ground,
To win has always been in all his dreams,
He shares the longing with his ride, it seems.

Creeping, creeping, slowly, slowly creeping,
The crowd are bellowing and some are weeping,
For joy or sorrow? That we do not know,
The final outcome of this race will show.
Can these two 'meet with triumph or disaster'?
Still they race towards the red disc, faster
Than anyone has ever seen before,
This is the race that no one will ignore.

Then suddenly, like firework, smoke and flame,
The horse that, before this, was just a name,
Has come back with a new astounding speed,
The race is now impossible to read,
The roars and shouts scream out that they are level,
Astonishing to angel or to devil,
The final cards of this game have been played,
The balance of victory is slowly swayed.

A flash of dark, dark bay, and conker red,
Are separated now just by a head,
Locked together, now that is what it seems,
And both are driven onward by their dreams,
To turn defeat into sweet victory,
And make their names go down in history,
Now Rummy leads: three quarters of a length,
And no one in the crowd has not drawn breath,
Now they cross the line! It's international!
Reporters scream, 'Red Rum has won the National!'

And dear old Rummy, does he understand?
Has he decided fate has played a hand?
As the jockey sits there, tired and bashful,
How does it feel to him to win the National?
As Rummy looks around, in his dark eyes,
There is only a twinkling of surprise,
Is this the thing he might have known before?
Who knows? His place in history is secure.

Anusia Battersby (14)

FOUR CHILDHOOD MEMORIES

My first childhood memory was when I was three
My brother was sitting in his high chair laughing happily
His high chair was white with little green rocking chains
And behind him the room was a mess with toys and bears
The sun was shining on my happy brother
And in the doorway stood my beloved mother
My brother was like an angel sent from a cloud
Sent to cheer us up with his laugh, so very loud.

My second childhood memory was the very same year
And of going to nursery I had no fear
My dad, on his way to work, walked past
And to me it seemed he was walking very fast
I was sitting by the window playing with the toys
Listening to the playful laughter of other girls and boys
The sky was grey and it was going to rain
And my hair was as tuggy as a horse's mane.

My next memory was when I was five
And I walked into school nervously, not feeling alive
My twin sister and I got nervous as my mum and dad said goodbye
Me keeping my head down and rolling up the bottom of my tie
My classroom was yellow and bright
I slowly realised I would be alright
My teacher came to say hello
And told us to sit at the front of class in a neat little row.

My next and last memory
Was when I was in Primary Three
And I was playing with my friends
Not caring whether my shoes were of the latest trends
We were sitting against the fence eating our snacks
Moving every so often so the fence didn't dig into our backs
We were playing houses and families
But kept getting bothered by the hungry bees.

These are some of my childhood memories
Dating back to when I was three
They are little snapshots and videos in my mind
Always there for me to find.

Fiona Martin (12)

PERFECT POEM

A letter came through the post one morning,
For a poem I must write,
I sat there thinking for days and days,
And it kept me up all night!

What genre, structure, features to use,
Aha, I've got an idea,
Haikus, cinquains, syllables galore,
Don't want to do those, oh dear!

Caligram or shape poems,
What on earth are these,
Big or small, fat or thin,
Please help me, oh pretty please.

My aunt, sister, mum and gran
I was driving them crazy they said,
On the roof, up the stairs, back down again,
I felt like I was really dead.

My aunty said she didn't have time,
My sister said too boring,
Mum said, 'Later dear,'
And my gran started snoring!

I sat there, giving up,
I knew this wasn't fair,
I'll just do a poem on perfect poems,
While sitting in my chair.

Hmm . . . let's begin.

Nadia Khalid (10)

VALENTINE

Not a box of chocolates, nor a cuddly teddy,
I give you a cactus.
It is a deadly cucumber in a green mantle,
It promises new life,
Like the unfolding of love.

Here,
It will tear you with its needles
Like a drug,
It will make your laughter
Become an everlasting nightmare.

I am trying to be realistic!
Not a bouquet or a candlelight dinner
Its monstrous shadow,
Will make your heart stop and think twice.
Déjà vu.

Take it!
Its spiny layer warns you
Of danger in love.
Poison!

Its venomous drink will leave you desolated!

Zainab Khalid (13)

UNTITLED #2

It's the same song to a different beat,
My words could write themselves whilst I sleep,
They come alive in my head and just play loud,
I've tried sleeping with a pen and a pad,
Anything I could to get them spoken out,
I've tried to make them perfect,
I've tried to make them better,
Nothing's been worth it but now there's you,
And as I write this I know you're smiling
And my heart snaps in two
Because I know that smile isn't for me and you
And as I try that bit harder I'm waiting in the wings
Hoping the show doesn't begin.

Nathan Platts (15)

THE PICTURE

There was a beautiful picture in the room.
It stood out from the gloom.
It was of a man in grand old fashioned clothes,
Leaning on a table.
He looked like he was very able.
The light from the picture pulled me in.
I was almost knocked into a bin.
When I was finally whisked away.
Gosh, this was an amazing day
As I reflected on that perfect day
And on my bouncy bed I lay,
I thought *wow!*

Edward Samuelson (11)

LOVE

Love is great,
Love is true,
The sweetness of saying
'I love you'

True love is so pure,
And it twists your heart,
It just hits you
Like a flying dart

Love looks like a passionate rose,
Tastes like a cherry drop,
Fills your heart with happiness,
Makes you want to skip, jump and hop!

Cassylda Augusto-Rodrigues (11)

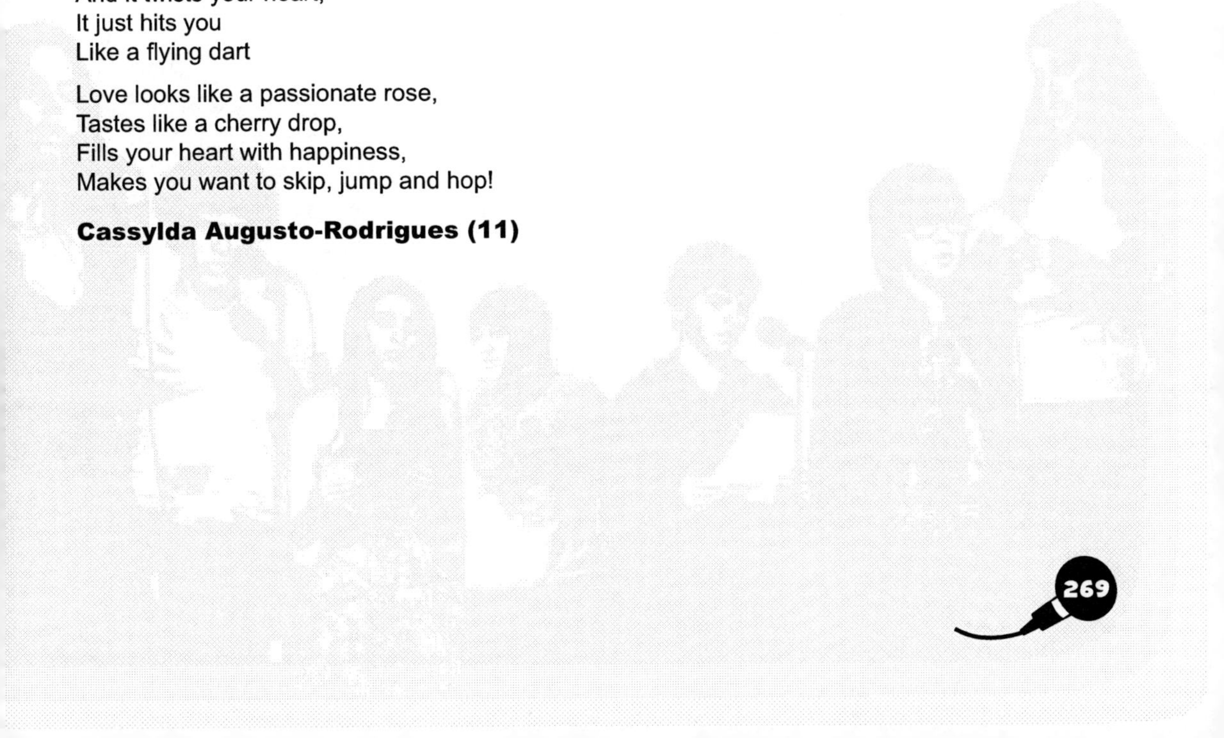

OUTCAST

I'm out of the crowd,
I can't help but shed a tear,
I'm shouting so loud but no one can hear.
They don't want to listen,
And neither do I,
They pretend to understand but I hate when they lie,
In my head I'm screaming,
I feel like stone inside,
There's never anyone in whom I can confide,
There's a feeling that I can't control,
A darkness in my mind,
I wish that I could start again and leave it all behind.

I used to think there was always hope,
But I'm losing faith in that illusion,
The ache in me takes over, the longing for inclusion.
They laugh when they see me,
They loathe my face and voice,
If only I had the confidence to help myself with choice.
The second I start flying,
I'm let down yet again,
I just can't eradicate that deep oppressing pain.
When I try to make things better,
It never goes the right way for me,
Someone clear this darkness so that I can try to see.

The hurt that I am holding,
It's like nothing you've felt before,
I'm just stuck in this painful endless war.
The doors just keep on closing,
And there's never any light,
Now I have got no energy,
No energy left to fight.
My faith is fading fast,
I can't stay in this world of hate,
And I can easily guess the chance of my near fate.
My hint of a spark has now gone out,
The clouds have darkened and hidden the sun,
My life is lost and the battle is won.

Kerri Robinson (13)

STAYING HOPEFUL

When you are reading this poem you could be happy.
When you are reading this poem you could be sad.
But just think, it can't be that bad!
Always stride with your head up high and hope in your heart!
Never let you and your dreams get set apart!
Never give up no matter what you've got to do.
Your friends and family are always there for you!
Some days will be high, some will be low,
But only dead fish go with the flow.

Iona Grant (13)

HER FAVOURITE GAME

Snarling and baring a jaw full of knives,
Hissing and flicking her tongue in and out,
No innocent victim ever survives,
She just bites you more if you try to shout.

Waiting to pounce on your slightest wrong move,
Her meaty breath burns the back of your neck,
Why you deserve it she will never prove,
She's enormous and you are a dirty speck.

You cower when her gaping nostrils flare,
Her fiery blazing eyes turn you to stone,
She'll penetrate you with her icy stare,
Make you shiver and chill you to the bone.

You whisper or breathe and her ears prick up,
Her long curling claws dig into your flesh,
She slurps her drink from her 'best teacher' cup,
She chews on something that doesn't look fresh.

Bullying is her top favourite game,
Her vicious tongue is hurtful, often cruel,
Children and rats in her mind are the same,
That is why her class dread going to school.

Philippa Louise Crundwell (13)

PANIC ATTACK

I didn't know what to do
I didn't know how to act
Nobody likes anything new
Round here that's a fact
It probably is with you too

I felt so short of breath
My fingers were viciously numb
I thought it would lead to death
So scared of the outcome

The world was spinning round
Round and round my head
I felt so very unsafe
The cure still hidden and unsaid

My mouth was like a desert
Deadly and inhumanly dry
I was shaking like an earthquake
Yet nothing to destroy nearby

My stomach was aching so badly
Which is when it started to go good
I looked up so very sadly
And that's where a teacher stood

I was given a piece of advice
The only advice that was known
Just calm down and breathe very deeply
Given in a calming tone

I tried to calm down,
But there was only one phrase I could handle
And I have no idea why
'Just smell the roses and blow out the candles'

So that's what I did
I followed my instructions
And all of a sudden I could breathe again
And breathing became a part of my productions

In the end I was sent home
I couldn't go by bus
I just refused to be alone
I was told it was a panic attack
And that just made me fuss.

Jenny Aimee Nzabandora (12)

UNTITLED

The harmonies of our heartbeats stain their callous souls.
The fiery yearn unfolds inside our minds as it does theirs.
The same passions; the same excitements flourish in them
As they do in us to their foolish misconceptions.

The government compile the bills and sign the sheets of paper
Thinking that their conducts will suffice. And yet, they,
Who rarely look past their ego - witness our torture:
Across the street, late at night, in that very alley way.

Many two-faced politicians secretly agree.
What makes *you* so different from my people and me?

Our hearts have the capacity to feel pain. So do yours.
Our eyes can distinguish black from white. So can yours.
Our souls are born angelic, not demonic. So are yours.
Our appearances differ. We're not perfect; we have flaws.

We're really not that different! We don't wish to even scores!
Accept us. Please. We wish to end all wars.

Beth Sheerin (14)

PIGEONS, PIGEONS!

Pigeons, pigeons everywhere!
On the walls, on the chairs!
Eating scraps everywhere!
Staring at me, I'm so scared!
But I'm just in Trafalgar Square!

Saaqib Asif-Jussab (12)

LAST YEAR

After four years of hard work the time has come to leave,
The memories of the fun times we've had will always stay with me!
My form has been the best, we've had some great times,
Like when we played 'Michael Jackson - The Experience'
On the Nintendo Wii!

Last few days, watching movies and chilling out!
Next year, no uniform! We can wear what we want without a doubt!

Once again we'll be the youngest as we move on to a new school,
New people, new teachers, new classes, new rules.

Final reports out, with our end of Key Stage grades,
GCSEs from now on and I hope I get some As!

Sports Day, Induction Day and the prom . . . sorry leavers' ball!
End of year trip to Alton Towers will be a fun time for us all!

I'll miss the class assemblies, (especially ours) as they were so much fun!
Awards assemblies coming up, then time at high school for us, is gone.

Biding farewell to my teachers, form and my other friends.
I can't believe how fast the year has gone and soon is going to end!

After four years of hard work the time has come to leave,
The memories of the fun times I've had will always stay with me!
My form has been the best, we've had some great times,
Like when we played 'Michael Jackson - The Experience'
On the Nintendo Wii!

Azrah Asif-Jussab (14)

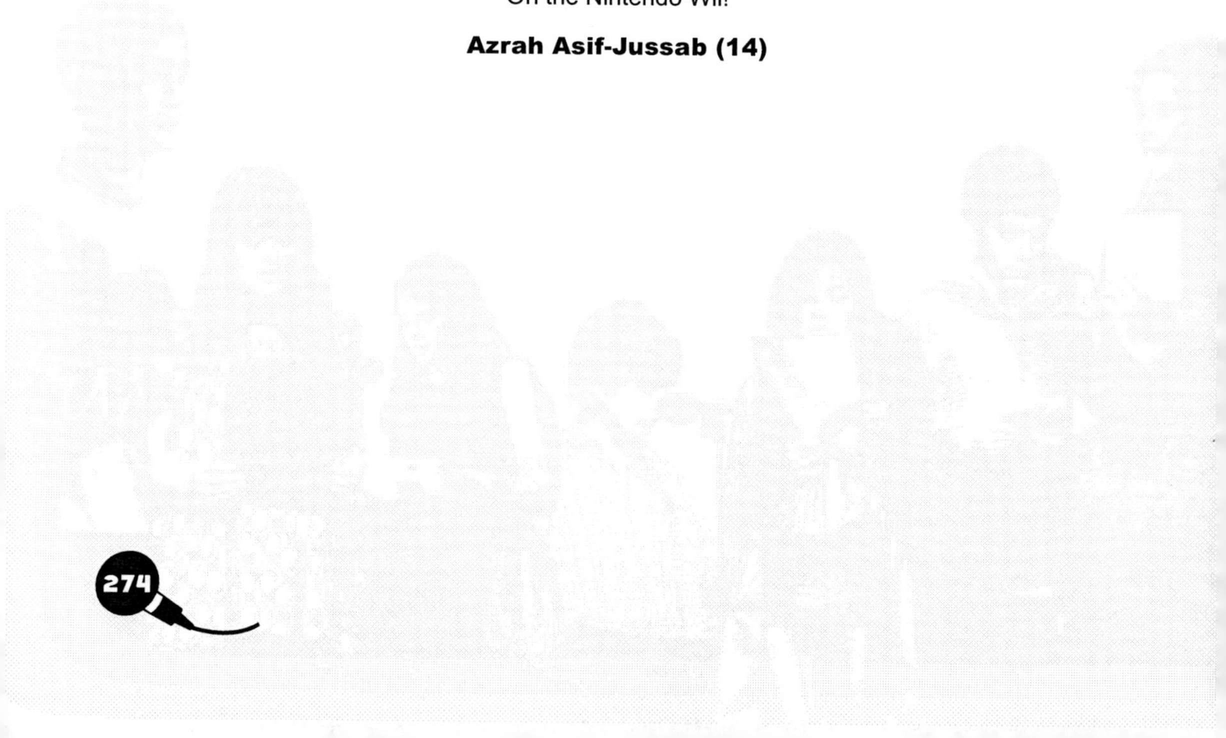

ME TO YOU

The sun is yellow, water is blue,
This poem is written from me to you.
Leaves are green, clouds are white,
One of the colours on a colourful kite.
Tree trunks are brown,
I know this because I see them all over the town.
Vegetables grow deep down below,
Waiting to pop up and say hello.
The sun is yellow, water is blue,
This poem is written from me to you.

Victoria Arku-Gilbertson (6)

HOURS, MINUTES, SECONDS

Nothing that exists can exist until the end of time,
but can time exist if there is nothing existing to fill an empty void?
When we sleep and dream even,
are we simply resting our bodies
or perhaps our lives?
We may seem to die at the end of our existence
but does existing affect who we are?
Do we carry on under pressure of time
and do we exist to simply waste time?
Because existing is time but time does not exist without
existence.

Keri-Amber Forster (12)

ANIMALS

Life is like a house of animals
Dogs, cats, rats, snakes and pigs.
Dogs do what they want, while the cats run,
Rats look in awe, while living in sorrow.
Snakes secretly hate,
At the dogs and cats,
While they debate, how to degrade lives for these own sake.
The pigs do dirt,
But throw it in the rest of their faces.
It's disgusting.
They don't like dogs and cats.
The rats,
And the snakes are in line with the pigs.
The out of line swine,
That hate if you shine,
They'll hunt down the dogs,
Put cats on their line.
Thankfully ignore the rats,
But applaud the snakes.
Serpents the servants of swine,
Living the high life,
Reaping dirty benefits.
But for all whose benefit?
Because all dogs go to Heaven,
Cats play on the fiddle,
Rats get taken away while snakes slither away,
And the pigs get a clean,
Cut for their pork.

Kofi Dacres (16)

INDEX

FORWARD POETRY INFORMATION

We hope you have enjoyed reading this book - and that you will continue to enjoy it in the coming years.

If you like reading and writing poetry drop us a line, or give us a call, and we'll send you a free information pack.

Alternatively if you would like to order further copies of this book or any of our other titles, then please give us a call or log onto our website at www.forwardpoetry.co.uk.

Forward Poetry Information
Remus House
Coltsfoot Drive
Peterborough
PE2 9BF
(01733) 890099